G000275865

Christmas Evans

B. A. RAMSBOTTOM

ISBN 0 9510035 0 X

Published by
THE BUNYAN PRESS
23 Haslingden Close,
Harpenden, Herts AL5 3EW England
© 1985 B. A. Ramsbottom
4th Reprint 1994

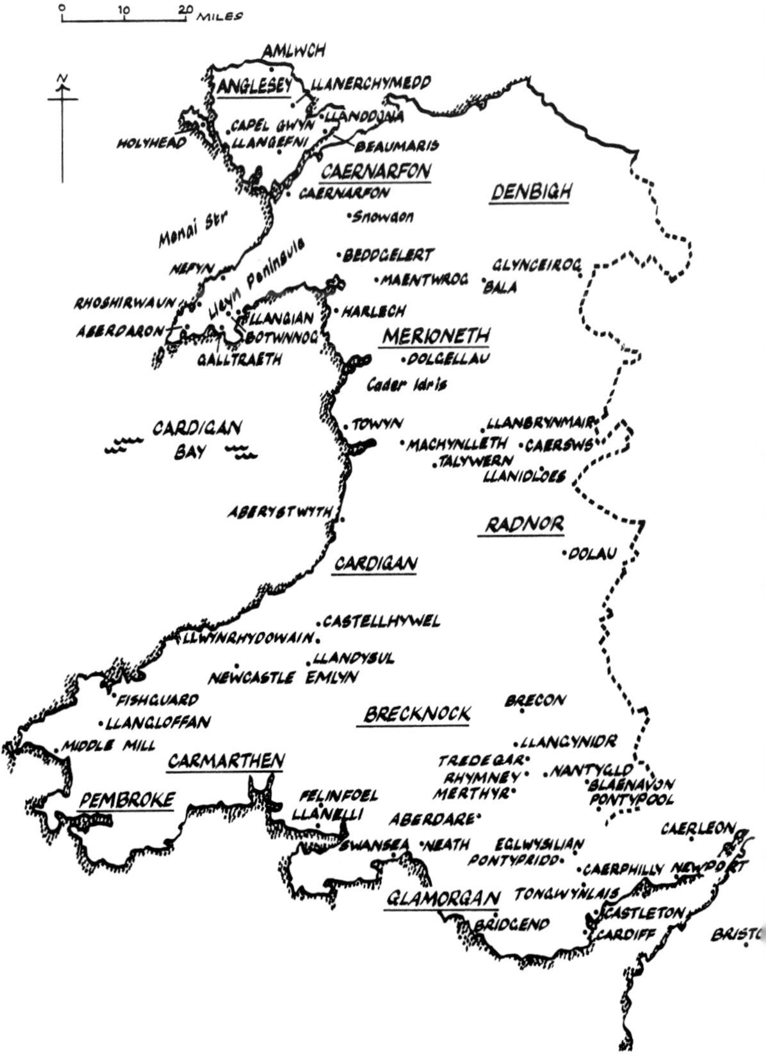

0
10
20
MILES
N
AMLWCH
ANGLESEY
LLANERCHYMEDD
CAPEL GWYN
LLANDDONA
HOLYHEAD
LLANGEFNI
BEAUMARIS
CAERNARFON
CAERNARFON
DENBIGH
Snowdon
Menai Str
Lleyn Peninsula
BEDDGELERT
NEFYN
MAENTWROG
GLYNCEIROG
BALA
RHOSHIRWAUN
HARLECH
LLANGIAN
ABERDARON
BOTWNNOG
MERIONETH
GALLTRAETH
DOLGELLAU
Cader Idris
TOWYN
LLANBRYNMAIR
CARDIGAN
BAY
MACHYNLLETH
CAERSWS
TALYWERN
LLANIDLOES
ABERYSTWYTH
RADNOR
DOLAU
CARDIGAN
CASTELLHYWEL
LLWYNRHYDOWAIN
LLANDYSUL
NEWCASTLE EMLYN
FISHGUARD
BRECON
BRECKNOCK
LLANGLOFFAN
LLANGYNIDR
MIDDLE MILL
CARMARTHEN
TREDEGAR
RHYMNEY
NANTYGLO
BLAENAVON
MERTHYR
PONTYPOOL
PEMBROKE
FELINFOEL
LLANELLI
ABERDARE
CAERLEON
SWANSEA
NEATH
EGLWYSILIAN
PONTYPRIDD
CAERPHILLY
NEWPORT
GLAMORGAN
TONGWYNLAIS
CASTLETON
BRIDGEND
CARDIFF

CONTENTS

Acknowledgements

The Publishers are grateful to Geoffrey Thomas of Aberystwyth for reading the script and checking the Welsh spellings. Usually the older spellings have been left *when they are in quotations* from the old writers. Hence the differences in places.

Black and white sketches are by Grace Parish.

Cover: Snowdon Horseshoe from Capel Curig. Photographed by Andy Williams – *Photographic Library*

CHRISTMAS EVANS

"The mightiest preacher of the age."
                    Dr. Thomas Raffles of Liverpool, early 19th century

"The great preacher."
                    Biography by D. Rhys Stephen, 1847

"Christmas Evans was a Paul in labour, a Bunyan in imagination, and a Whitefield in eloquence."
                    Religious Tract Society biography, mid 19th century

"Of the few distinguished Welsh preachers of whom it may be said without exaggeration that they are known to fame, Christmas Evans has acquired the widest celebrity."
                    Biography by D. M. Evans, 1863

"The renowned apostle of Wales."
                    Lecture by Thomas Phillips of Cardiff, 1878

"That great man, whose name occupies the foremost place among those of the leading preachers of Wales . . . the greatest preacher that God has ever given to Wales."
                    "Echoes from the Welsh Hills" by David Davies, 1883

"This remarkable man and truly eminent minister of the gospel of Christ . . . a household word throughout the Principality."
                    "Friendly Companion," 1897

"Three preachers stood out above the rest, and they were alike in many things. They were Christmas Evans, a Baptist; John Elias, a Calvinistic Methodist; and Williams of Wern, an Independent. Of these three Christmas Evans alone passed beyond the bounds of the Principality, and established a name and reputation that were world-wide. His name became a household word among Christians everywhere."
                    Biography by E. Eberard Rees, c. 1936

"The great Christmas Evans, whom some would say was the greatest preacher that the Baptists have ever had in Great Britain."
                    Puritan Conference Address by Dr. D. M. Lloyd-Jones, 1967

CHAPTER 1

The Forgotten Christmas

It was a beautiful August evening when we set out in search of Christmas Evans's preaching place at Galltraeth at the back of Rhiw mountain. Leaving the main Aberdaron road at Botwnnog, we followed a minor road, and turning from this, a track which led toward the mountain side. Abandoning the car we pressed on, armed with detailed instructions and an Ordnance Survey map. Still there was no sight of Christmas Evans's chapel.

Eventually we knocked at the door of a remote farmstead. A fierce-looking, bearded man answered and received us very kindly. Yes, he knew about Christmas Evans. (Had not camera men been up taking a film only a week or two ago?) Quickly he explained to us where the chapel stood, adding, "And up on the hillside is a well, where he got his holy water!" How mysterious the legends that have arisen about both ancient and modern saints!

Thanking our kind informer for his help, we began to leave, when he called: "Just one thing! Do you mind going round the other side of the farm? It is a miracle you ever got in. The billy-goat is better than any watch dog!"

We found the old ruined chapel, almost secluded by trees, with a burial ground which must have been used as recently as the last war. This was truly "wild Wales." Behind the chapel rose the mountain. In the other direction the sea at Porth Neigwl was clearly visible.

The sun sank behind the mountains. Here and there a bat flitted past us. The wind began to blow cold. Yet there was something hallowed about the setting.

We had long felt that Christmas Evans was both a great man and a very gracious man and now there was a wish that once again people should know of "the forgotten Christmas."

ABERDARON

CHAPTER 2

Cwmtywyll: The Dark Valley

The long, straggling Mid Welsh village of Llandysul (nearly ten miles from Newcastle Emlyn) lies near a wild, mountainous tract of country which has been described as "a scene of the wildest magnificence." Here over two hundred years ago, at a place called Ysgarwen, lived a poor shoemaker, Samuel Evans, with his wife Johanna. The 25th of December, 1766, was to be a special day to them. They were anxiously awaiting the birth of a baby (their second) and before nightfall a son was born to them. Because of the day of his birth he was given a special name – Christmas. Of his father we know nothing except that he was always fighting sickness; of his mother we have just one mention: the fact that she urged Christmas, when a little boy, to think of his eternal welfare, eliciting the comment that she was a good preacher! Whatever memories he had of his parents he never made known to others; it was a common trait among Welsh people at this time to be very reticent about their family affairs.

There was nothing in Christmas Evans's humble beginnings to suggest any other lot than that of his parents, that he should live and die in obscurity and poverty. But God had intended otherwise.

Much of the Wales into which he was born was still sunk in deep ignorance and gross superstition (the belief in "corpse candles" and the like – strange lights seen when a person died) yet there were few districts entirely untouched by the revival under the preaching of the great Daniel Rowland.

While Christmas was only a child his poor father died and his widow with her little family had to struggle hard against poverty and even destitution. When what seemed a wonderful opening appeared, she was only too glad to seize it. Her brother, James Lewis, had a farm at a place named Bwlchog in the nearby parish of Llanfihangel-ar-arth and promised to take little Christmas and feed and clothe him in return for any duties on the farm he could perform.

Christmas spent six years with his uncle – six years of sadness and misery. He had to look after his uncle's cattle at Cwmtywyll – meaning "the dark valley," a very significant name. His Uncle James proved to be a selfish drunkard and most cruel man. In fact in later life Christmas Evans said of his uncle: "It would be difficult to find a more unconscionable man than James Lewis in the whole course of a wicked world." His uncle's only care seemed to be to get as much work out of him with the smallest possible expense. During these impressionable years, no care was taken of him either morally or religiously or to give him the rudiments of education. At the age of seventeen he could not read a single word.

Yet during these sorrowful years a merciful

A WELSH COTTAGE

providence was watching over him – a fact which left a deep impression on him in later years. Several times he almost lost his life. Once he was dangerously stabbed in the chest in a quarrel with another herdsboy. On another occasion he was nearly drowned after falling into a deep pool and only rescued with difficulty. On yet another occasion a horse ran away with him, galloping through a low, narrow passage so that he might well have been crushed to death. But perhaps his most remarkable deliverance was when he fell from a high tree with an open knife in his hand, remaining unconscious till helped by a passer by. Who cannot fail to see God's watchful care in all this?

In later years there was a story abroad that Christmas Evans had been a boxer but, in fact, he

11

never fought a battle in his life! Yet he grew up "without God and without hope in the world," associated only with things low and brutal.

When about seventeen years of age he left his uncle. He is described, at this time, as being specially uncouth and awkward – "a large-boned, muscular, much brooding and somewhat passionate young man." Not exactly a flattering description!

Still working as a farmer's boy he moved to Glanclettwr, then Penyralltfawr, then Gwenawlt, then Castellhywel. His days were spent in dire poverty, without friend and without home. But the time had come when God would begin His work in Christmas Evans's heart.

CHAPTER 3

A New Life

God's sovereignty is most mysterious. Often He uses the most unusual means to accomplish His purposes. So it was with the conversion of Christmas Evans.

At Llwynrhydowain stood a Presbyterian chapel. The minister, David Davies, a great, unwieldy figure, clothed with loose-fitting garments and crowned with flaxen hair (his size was prodigious) was a man of considerable classical attainment, and was renowned as a Welsh bard. Yet his views of the Person of the Lord Jesus were very faulty. A man of great kindness, his loose views of truth sprang from a desire to be easy, rather than from any critical spirit. When an old man he heard a "sound" sermon by the eminent minister "Williams of Wern" and exclaimed, "If that sermon be true, it will be a dark look out for a great many of us."

Yet here at Llwynrhydowain, about the year 1783, a revival of religion broke out. Many young people appeared to be graciously affected, and united with the church, Christmas Evans being one of them. Of these converts Christmas Evans said: "What became of the major part of these young converts I have never known, but I hope God's grace followed them as it did me, the meanest of them all."

Sadly we have no details of Christmas's spiritual experience at this time, though he tells us that even from his ninth year "the fear of death and of the day of judgment greatly agitated me; so much so that, after a certain fashion, I offered many a prayer. These moods, however, did not last long, but came now and then – and vanished." Concerning the change at this time his own judgment in later days was not too favourable; yet in his old age he said:

> "The fear of dying in an ungodly state especially affected me (even from childhood), and this apprehension clung to me till I was induced to rest upon Christ. All this was accompanied by some little knowledge of the Redeemer; and now, in my seventieth year, I cannot deny that this concern was the dawn of the day of grace on my spirit, although mingled with much darkness and ignorance."

Even from his spiritual infancy he was blessed with a spirit of prayer:

> "The spirit of energetic supplication was given to me early. A sense of danger prompts the soul to seek deliverance. Earnestness in prayer grew with me, though I frequently feared it would become extinct. Still, it was not entirely extinguished, even in those days of darkness when I but barely perceived that the merits of Christ were the only plea, without reference to anything of our own. After I came to know and feel that the righteousness of Christ formed the only ground to be depended upon before God, I was able with every sense

A WELSH COTTAGE KITCHEN

of unworthiness to approach Him with a stronger expectation. The Christian must have a rock in the merits of the Redeemer to rest upon; and here he finds 'a place of refuge, and a covert from the storm and the rain.'"

According to the popular account Christmas Evans very early had to suffer for Jesus' sake. Having now been compelled to separate from all his wicked friends and acquaintances, he had to prove their bitterness against his Master and against himself. He had just bought a copy of *The Pilgrim's Progress* and, as he journeyed home, paused from time to time to read a few sentences. Suddenly six of his former companions waylaid him, beat him unmercifully, whilst one hit him in the eye with a stick – as a result of which the eye was lost. In later years he was known as "the one-eyed preacher of Wales" but even from his youth he could say with Paul, "I bear in my body the marks of the Lord Jesus." And all this simply because he was turned from sin to God.* Strangely, Christmas Evans's brother, who spent his life almost as a tramp, looked remarkably like his brother and he too had lost an eye – how, we do not know.

Though his pastor's preaching was deficient in the truth, he showed the greatest interest in Christmas Evans. Persons blessed with grace are seldom content to remain ignorant and Christmas was no exception. He thirsted for knowledge. A few of the young men bought Bibles and candles and used to meet together in a barn at Penyralltfawr. Referring to himself and others at this time he says:

> "We had but little knowledge of the way of salvation, and less experience of it in our hearts; but many who were not able to read a word before now became so anxious to learn that they were soon able to read the Scriptures. I should suppose that up to this time not one out of seven persons in these districts knew how to read."

No wonder that later he said, "The Bible is the Book of books, a Book breathed out of heaven . . . I am very thankful for books written by man, but it is God's Book that sheds the light of life everlasting on all other books." In a month he could read the Bible in Welsh and then he borrowed books to learn a little English.

* It is only fair to say that another account does not connect the loss of his eye with suffering for Jesus' sake but rather with a period of backsliding. A third account connects the two: in a backsliding state he had gone to a fair, but coming away was assaulted because of his Christian profession.

16

Eventually Mr. Davies, realising the boy's enthusiasm, took him to his school for six months. Quite a remarkable story is told of how this came about. One evening Christmas asked John, the senior farm hand, if he could go to hear his pastor (and master – the farm on which he worked belonged to Mr. Davies) preach the following Sabbath. John gladly gave permission, promising to look after the sheep and cattle for him.

Throughout the service Christmas sat with his head buried in his hands, and as soon as the service was over hastened home without a word to anyone. After a quick dinner he was out among the sheep to relieve John.

David Davies could not help noticing the young man's unusual behaviour. After dinner he sent for John and asked him about Christmas Evans. "He is a strange boy!" he added. But John said, "You come with me." Together, quietly, they crept into the field and there Christmas was busy preaching the morning sermon (almost word for word) to a congregation of cows, horses and sheep.

On the way home Mr. Davies asked, "Do you know where I can get a boy to take the place of Christmas?" The boy was soon found and that evening John told Christmas he would no longer be needed to look after his sheep. This news was received with sorrow. What had he done to deserve to be dismissed? But his master soon relieved his fears: "You are to come to my school. You shall be educated free of charge."

Though there were many defects in David Davies's theology, there was a natural discernment (and also kindliness) which made him single Christmas Evans out for what help could be given.

Here he learned Latin grammar, but it was not possible for his education to be continued for longer than six months.

CHAPTER 4

The Young Preacher

Very early in his Christian life Christmas Evans seemed to be concerned about preaching. The night after he suffered the loss of his eye, he had a remarkable dream. The day of judgment was come and the world was in a blaze, yet with confidence he cried, "Jesus, save me!" In his dream it seemed as if the Lord turned towards him and said, "It was thy intention to preach the gospel, but now it is too late for the day of judgment is come." When he awoke, his dream clung to him. Throughout his life Christmas Evans had many remarkable impressions through dreams, and believed that God spoke to him in this way.

From the time of that dream there was a deep concern that he should preach. There were, however, obstacles in the way. There was a rule connected with the church where he was a member that no-one should be permitted to preach till he had passed

EIGHTEENTH CENTURY WELSH CHAPEL

through a college course.

It is an interesting fact that the night Christmas Evans was received into church membership, another young man who was to become an eminent minister was received at the same time. This was David Davies (the same name as their pastor), afterwards of Swansea. Their first pastor always regretted in after years that, because of the rule concerning preaching in their church, two of Wales's greatest preachers were lost to their denomination. It is also interesting to recall that both the young men preached their first sermons in the same cottage in the same week.

Cottage preaching was of far more importance in bygone Wales than many today could realise, and the congregations which met in those old Welsh cottages were very discerning.

It was at one of these cottage meetings that Christmas Evans first preached. The cottage belonged to a kind tailor who taught singing classes in the neighbourhood, and who helped the young men to learn to read. However, to say the least, his beginnings were not very auspicious. With a desire to do well, his first sermon was taken from Bishop Beveridge's *Thesaurus Theologicus* (most probably borrowed from his pastor). The sermon seemed to make some impression – till a farmer who was among the hearers went home and found the very book (and sermon) on his shelves! (What a witness, incidentally, to the knowledge, even intellectualism, among the old Welsh rural society! Which of us have read *Thesaurus Theologicus?*) In later years, this "stealing sermons" was a practice which became rather common in Wales, but against which Christmas Evans vehemently protested!

Thus the poor boy's reputation as a preacher seemed gone. "Still," said the good farmer, "I have some hope of the son of Samuel the shoemaker because the prayer was as good as the sermon." Perhaps he would have thought otherwise had he known that the prayer likewise was borrowed – from a collection of prayers by Griffith Jones of Llanddowror.

But "the lad Christmas, Samuel the shoemaker's son," was encouraged by one or two Baptist and Independent ministers in the locality, and occasionally preached for them, especially for Mr. Perkins, the Independent minister at Pencader, who showed him much kindness and sympathy, and often had him to preach in his pulpit.

But, at this time, he was often in agony of soul concerning his own state before God, no doubt due to the "uncertain sound" of his own pastor's ministry. The tendency of what he heard preached was to encourage self-righteousness, whilst he himself was bitterly conscious of his own guilt and corruption.

Yet this was to be the man of whom it would be said in later years: "He helped to fill Wales with the radiance of the pure gospel."

CHAPTER 5

Baptism – and Timothy Thomas

God never leaves His work unfinished. We are not, then, surprised to discover that as Christmas Evans was led by the Holy Spirit more deeply into the truth, he became dissatisfied with the erroneous preaching of his first pastor. Apart from the false views on the Deity of Christ, he could not be satisfied with Arminianism or with legality of any kind. He began to hear preachers, some of whom were giants of the faith, who had clear views of divine truth, and so he was led into more gracious views of the Person and finished work of Christ, and the doctrine of justification by faith.

As he grew in grace, he became haunted with tremendous fears and said he felt his heart to be "a little hell within him." During many seasons of deep darkness and depression, he learned the secret of self-distrust. He became increasingly attracted to people of Calvinistic views.

One of his fellow members was a man named Amos. Hearing that he had left the church and united with the Calvinistic Baptists, Christmas began to study the Word of God more carefully and was led to see that both in doctrine and in practice they were much nearer the Word of God. Their godliness of life and remarkable knowledge of the Scriptures also strongly attracted him to the great doctrines of the gospel which they professed. (A similar change took place in his young friend David Davies, but he joined the Independents.) Christmas Evans gives his own account:

"A person of the name of Amos had left the church at Llwynrhydowen, and had been baptized at Aberduar. He came to see me, and I began to assail the Anabaptist heresy, as I had been accustomed to consider it. But Amos soon silenced me. I attributed my defeat to my ignorance of the New Testament, and therefore began to read from the beginning of Matthew, to prepare myself for the next interview. Having read the New Testament through, I found not a single verse in favour of Paedobaptism (i.e. baptizing infants). I met frequently with passages in the Old and New Testaments referring to the circumcision and the naming of children, their bringing up in the 'nurture and admonition of the Lord,' etc., but with none making any mention of their baptism; while about forty passages seemed to me to testify clearly for baptism on a profession of faith. These scriptures spoke to my conscience, and convinced me of the necessity of personal obedience to the baptism which Christ had ordained. After a little struggle between the flesh and the spirit, obedience and disobedience, I applied to the Baptist church at Aberduar. I was cordially received, but not without some fear on my part that I was a rank Arminian still."

He was then about twenty years and six months old. (This would be in the summer of 1787.) He was baptized in the River Duar by Timothy Thomas. It would appear that a true revival was taking place at Aberduar at that time, and many were added to the church.

Christmas Evans's new pastor was a most remarkable man – a gentleman, living on a splendid farm, preaching and fulfilling the work of a pastor without any monetary reward. He was renowned for his noble appearance, his independent spirit and his generosity. Each Saturday he would ride thirty or forty miles through the wilds of Carmarthenshire and Cardiganshire to be ready for the Lord's day services. Often when preaching or baptizing in the open air, the mobs that assembled to cause a disturbance were overcome by his gentlemanly bearing – some fearing he was at least a magistrate.

But he was also a man of very clear theological views. A beautiful story shows us what calibre of man he was. On one occasion one of his church members was brought up on a case of discipline; he had knocked a man down. On enquiry it appeared that the man, a Unitarian, had said some blasphemous things about the Person of Christ and His precious blood. This had proved too much and, losing control of himself, the Baptist member had knocked him down. Timothy Thomas carefully listened to all the circumstances and then dismissed the case, wryly remarking, "Well, I cannot say you did the right thing – but I quite believe I should have done the same! Go, and sin no more."

Such was Christmas Evans's new pastor, and it is little wonder that under such a man and such a ministry he became more established in the truth. The noble old gentleman died at the age of 86. When in his old age he was asked, "How many have you baptized?" he would reply, "I have baptized at least two thousand; and thirty of them have become ministers of the gospel. And I baptized Christmas Evans."

EIGHTEENTH CENTURY WELSH FARMHOUSE

CHAPTER 6

Llŷn: A Gale of Grace

Martin Luther said that prayer, meditation and temptation are the things that make a minister. This waiting time, a time of deep exercise, was a time of sore temptation for Christmas Evans. Often he suffered deep spiritual depression. He knew he must preach but felt himself a mass of ignorance and sin. He was grieved by his first attempt in the cottage. Then, committing his own sermons to memory, he felt he had forfeited the help of the Holy Spirit. Attempting the opposite and preaching without any premeditation at all, he said:

> "But this was a change from bad to worse; I had neither sense, warmth, nor life, nothing but a poor weakly intonation that could impress no one. I thought that God would have nothing to do with me as a preacher, or in any other way, but that I was altogether a mass of carnality. The sound of my own voice, in praying or in preaching, disheartened me, as it seemed to proceed

from a hard heart. I regarded every other preacher as worthy of his office, but I had no faith in myself. I had no confidence in my knowledge of the Bible; I believed that everyone excelled me.

"Since then I have had a deep sense of divine goodness in all this, for it preserved me, while a young man, from a vain conceit of my own gifts, which has, before and since, been the shipwreck of many. I had no friend on earth to whom I could reveal the plague of my heart. I dared not make known my secret feelings, for fear that, in case they were known, it should be decided that I was still an unconverted man, and that it would become the talk of the whole neighbourhood."

So his deep exercises continued, and he was daily humbled. Conscious of his unusual appearance he was tempted that his mere standing in the pulpit was enough to becloud his hearers' hearts. Then he had no close friend to whom he could unbosom his cares, but felt that if he tried to speak to anyone, he would immediately appear a hypocrite. So his heart knew its own bitterness. Yet through these painful experiences his God was preparing him for his life's work.

What a lesson there is here! He was a member of a church where much joy abounded into which he himself could not enter. Day by day he went about in heaviness of spirit. Yet he was the one who was being specially prepared for the greatest usefulness. "For half a century," writes David Rhys Stephen, he was to "preach the gospel with zeal, ability and power unsurpassed in his day." As a result of his deep burden of soul and later deliverance, he was able with truth and gratitude to say, "Blessed be God, even the Father of our Lord Jesus Christ, the Father of mercies, and the God of all comfort; who comforteth us in all our tribulation, that we may be able to

LAND'S END OF LLŶN

comfort them which are in any trouble, by the comfort wherewith we ourselves are comforted of God."

At the age of twenty-three several ministers at the Association meetings at Maesyberllan in Breconshire besought him to move to the Llŷn peninsula (or, as it is often known, Lleyn) and he was ordained as a "missionary" to preach among the humble churches there. There had been some blessing in the north of Wales following the labours of Dr. Thomas Llewellyn in 1776, but there was a great need of ministers. The peninsula is still one of the most unspoiled parts of the British Isles, majestic in the beauty of its wild hills and mountains, clad with heather and gorse, and its delightful beaches. Its wildness and remoteness two hundred years ago can only be imagined (more than ten days journey from London). Yet wildness and remoteness bring their own difficulties. It has been quaintly said: "Mountains keep back advancing man, be he soldier or preacher." And superstition still reigned. An English traveller recorded: "At Clynnog Fawr the people come to bathe in Saint Beuno's Well, and the children are left to sleep on the tomb after bathing, for the rickets, this being a part of the cure." Daniel Rowlands and Howell Harris on many occasions nearly lost their lives for the truth's sake in "wild Wales."

It would appear that Christmas proceeded straight from the Association meetings at Maesyberllan to Llŷn, without even returning home to say goodbye. With much fear he went, preaching along his journey as opportunity arose. D. M. Evans comments:

> "The route from Maesyberllan through Llanbrynmair, Dolgellau, and Harlech, into Carnarvonshire, lay through some of the grandest scenery, then comparatively unknown to the throngs of tourists which now invade these peaceful solitudes; and had our young traveller furnished us with any notes of the impressions produced upon him, the first time he found himself where nature in his native land assumes her wildest shapes and most awful moods, they would have been deeply interesting."

Up till this time Christmas Evans's ministry does not seem to have made any special mark in his own neighbourhood, but as soon as he moved to Llŷn a new life seems to have begun. It was at this time he was brought into the full light and liberty of the gospel. He himself made a note:

> "I then felt that I died to the law, abandoned all hope of preparing myself to apply to the Redeemer, and realised the life of faith and dependence on the righteousness of Christ for my justification."

From the beginning a wonderful power attended his preaching, and numbers were blessed and gathered into the church. During his first year he baptized fifty persons at Tynydonen, and eighty persons sought membership the second year, though many of these, because of their family connections, joined the Calvinistic Methodists. Years after he left Llŷn one of their deacons told him, "Droves of your spiritual children are in our societies to this day."

The theme of his preaching was free and sovereign grace, and it is recorded that "a new and experimental knowledge of the way of salvation lighted up his ministry."

"I could scarcely believe," he says, "the testimony of the people who came before the church as candidates for membership, that they were converted through my ministry; yet I was obliged to believe, though it was marvellous in my eyes. This made me thankful to God, and increased my confidence in prayer. A delightful gale descended upon me as from the hill of the New Jerusalem, and I felt the three great things of the kingdom of heaven: righteousness, and peace, and joy in the Holy Ghost."

His burden seemed rolled away. Surely it was at this time that he learned truths like the following:

"Holiness, righteousness and purity look at me out of the midst of the Book, like the fires of Sinai in Israel, or the I AM out of the burning bush, causing me to fear and tremble, while I am yet desirous of looking at the radiant glory because it is tempered with mercy. I take my shoes off my feet, and approach on my knees to see this great sight. I cannot live in sin in this presence; still it does not slay me. The eternal power is here, and with one hand it conceals me in the shadow of redeeming mercy, and with

31

the other it points out the glory of the great and wondrous truth that God is at once a just God and the Justifier of him that believeth in Jesus."

Frequently, like Daniel Rowland and Howell Harris before him, he preached out of doors, and frequently found his congregation bathed in tears. Remarkable was the change in the religious life of the district – from coldness and deadness to life and power. Of books he had few: his Bible, possibly some of Bunyan's works, a borrowed Welsh–English dictionary, and Burkitt on the New Testament, which he would study in bed at night, looking up all the hard words in the dictionary.

Here in Llŷn Christmas Evans was strongly influenced by Robert Roberts of Clynnog (1762–1802), a popular preacher whose preaching was followed by marked effects. He was also a man of prayer, and it was said that he had even arrested storms by his prayers. Christmas Evans was once asked if he could give any reason for how he came into his unusual way of preaching. He replied:

"Yes, I can, partly at least; I had the ideas before, but somehow couldn't get at them. When I was in Llŷn, the Methodists (i.e. Calvinistic Methodists) had a preacher of the name of Robert Roberts, of Llanllyfni, who was very popular, and there was a great deal of talk about him. Well, I went on one Sunday afternoon to hear him. He was one of the most insignificant-looking persons I ever saw – a little, hunchbacked man; but he neither thought nor said anything like other people; there was something wonderful and uncommon about him. This Robert Roberts gave me the key."

It may be asked, What *was* Christmas Evans's

peculiar way of preaching? A short sample may be the best answer.

SAUL OF TARSUS AND HIS SEVEN SHIPS

"Saul of Tarsus was once a thriving merchant and an extensive shipowner. He had seven vessels of his own: the names of which were – 'Circumcised the eighth day'; 'Of the stock of Israel'; 'Of the tribe of Benjamin'; 'An Hebrew of the Hebrews'; 'As touching the law, a Pharisee'; 'Concerning zeal, persecuting the church'; 'Touching the righteousness which is of the law, blameless.' The sixth was a man-of-war with which he set out one day from the port of Jerusalem, well supplied with ammunition from the arsenal of the chief priest, with a view to destroy a small fort at Damascus.

"He was wonderfully confident, and breathed out threatenings and slaughter. But he had not gone far from port before the gospel ship, with Jesus Christ Himself as Commander on board, hove in sight, and threw such a shell among the merchant's fleet that all his ships were instantly on fire. The commotion was tremendous; and there was such a volume of smoke that Saul couldn't see the sun at noon.

"While the ships were fast sinking, the Gospel Commander mercifully gave orders that the perishing merchant should be taken on board. 'Saul, Saul, what has become of thy ships?' 'They are all on fire!' 'What wilt thou do now?' 'O that I may be found in Him, not having mine own righteousness, which is of the law, but that which is through the faith of Christ, the righteousness which is of God by faith.'"

It is little wonder that, on account of his allegorical way of preaching, he became known as "the Bunyan of Wales."

CHAPTER 7

The Presence of God

Soon after Christmas Evans began to preach in Llŷn he married one of his godly young church members, Catherine Jones, and in every way she was suited for the young minister's wife. It seems impossible how she managed, yet it is astonishing what she contrived to make out of oatmeal, buttermilk and potatoes – their staple diet.

There were five preaching places he supervised, scattered over the peninsula: Llangian; Tynydonen (Salem); Rhoshirwaun; Galltraeth; Nefyn. Often he preached five times on the Lord's day, travelling twenty miles, and after a time his arduous labours began to affect his health. He was exhausted, and consumption was suspected. Yet strangely he attempted a long preaching tour!

He set out towards Beddgelert to walk to South Wales and on the well-known road between the Aberglaslyn Pass and Maentwrog he had a wonderful blessing. This he later described to a friend on the very spot:

> "Although I had the gift of speaking, and was thirsting for knowledge that I might be able to teach others, and multitudes were eager to hear me, my fears (that God had not called him to the ministry) pressed so heavily upon me that I dismounted, fastened my horse, and went into a field close by (to pray), which I will just now point out to you; for as I draw near the place I recollect it more vividly. Whether anybody saw me I heeded not, because the end of all things, as it were, had come upon me. However, God had mercy on my poor soul, and I received Jacob's blessing; yes, I saw, as it were, the heavens open.
>
> "When I arose, I started on my journey, and the smiles of the heavenly Spirit lighted up my way for the space of two months. I have since that occasionally had my doubts and fears; but the fear that I had not been called to the ministry never afterwards so troubled me. I have not the slightest doubt but that it is my duty to put forth all my power in the ministry as long as I live."

He preached in every town and village through which he passed. (And it would appear that this strange medicine proved an effectual cure for his health!) As he moved farther south, large numbers of the same congregations would follow him the next day, and perhaps attend fifteen or twenty of his services altogether. So he went on through Cardigan, Pembroke, Carmarthen, Glamorgan, Monmouth and Brecon, and word went before him that a wonderful man of God had appeared. An announcement that Christmas Evans was to preach would attract crowds to the place. His own account is:

> "The chapels and burying-grounds were filled with people who crowded to hear me in the middle of harvest

time. In the evening I frequently preached in the open air, and the singing and rejoicing continued till broad daylight. Such a spirit of tenderness descended upon the hearers that they wept floods of tears and cried aloud. Whole multitudes, men and women, seemed melted by the power of the Word. The Word of God was now like a sharp two-edged sword, piercing through the joints and marrow, and discerning the thoughts and intents of the heart.

"I continued to be thus inspired wherever I went, so that preaching was a delight to me. The same people would gather to hear me fifteen or twenty times in the counties of Cardigan, Pembroke, Carmarthen, Glamorgan, Monmouth and Brecon. And the excitement then produced, especially in the districts of Cardigan and Pembrokeshire, inclined the whole country to think more favourably of religion.

A LLŶN SEASIDE VILLAGE

36

"The same heavenly breeze followed me down to Fishguard, Llangloffan and Rhydwilym, where Mr. Gabriel Rees was then a fervent preacher. From Tabor down to Middle-mill the people were so deeply affected that they wept and trembled like the aspen leaf; yet there was mixed up with this feeling so much heavenly enjoyment that they seemed to wish to abide in that state of mind for ever."

People have talked about Welsh emotion and the effect of beautiful singing but Christmas Evans normally closed the service with one single verse (usually by William Williams) which he gave out from memory. He always felt it was scriptural for him to conclude a service himself. There would be a short prayer, then his hymn, feelingly announced, and he would remain standing while the verse was sung.

But Christmas Evans only remained on the Llŷn peninsula for about two years. His reasons for leaving, after so much early prosperity, are various. Chiefly, it would seem, many who were blessed under his preaching did not become Baptists but joined the older, established and more flourishing chapels. The Baptists appear to have been disorderly and badly managed. But, to quote his own words:

"I cannot ascribe the low state of the Baptist denomination in Carnarvonshire to their views of the way of salvation, for on that subject they hold the same doctrines as the (Calvinistic) Methodists, who are in that county numerous and orderly. In their difference in regard to baptism, I conscientiously think that they are more in accordance with the Word of God than any others. God is pleased with their practice of a baptism which was acknowledged by the Father, Son and Holy Ghost in the river of Jordan (Matthew 3). But I attribute it (the low state of the churches), in the first place, to the precedency of the Methodists in that part of the country, and to the peculiarity of our views of baptism; secondly, to the want of suitable gifts and becoming character in several of the preachers who had laboured there; thirdly, to the lack of evangelical savour and unction in the ministry, and the presence of a sour and bigoted spirit; fourthly, to the want of exemplary piety in the members; fifthly, to the want of practical wisdom in the management of the affairs of the churches."

And it has been said, not unkindly, that though Christmas Evans was one of the greatest preachers, he was one of the worst administrators!

CHAPTER 8

Anglesey, "The Dark Isle"

In 1792 Christmas Evans left Llŷn. He had received what he calls a "providential intimation" that he should move to the island of Anglesey. The "providential intimation" was a call to serve all the Baptist churches on the island and his salary would be £17 a year! One John Jones of Nantglyn, from that island, came to Llŷn to invite him. He was to remain on the island for nearly thirty-four years; for years his salary never rose above the 6s 6½d (33p) a week, neither did he ever ask for more. Mr. Jones promised him the £17 "am wasanaethu Môn" – "for serving Anglesey": the whole island! And at this time the "Dark Isle," as it was known, was about the most heathenish part of Wales, noted for both smuggling and the plundering of wrecked vessels.

It was his birthday, Christmas Day, a very rough, frosty, snowy day, when he and his wife set out, both travelling on the back of the same horse. In the evening of the same day they reached Llangefni, where his home was to be. In those days it was scarcely a village – just a few scattered houses. Most of the houses consisted of just one room – where the family was born, where it lived, where it slept and where it died. In it all the washing, cooking, baking, weaving, spinning and dyeing were done. Hidden away in corners were the few belongings necessary to live, while under the rafters hung dried fish, salted meat and bacon, and the herbs so necessary to flavour the meals.

Cildwrn chapel was where he was to preach, but also to nine other congregations, all without chapels and meeting in private houses. He was their only minister, his nearest companion in his own denomination being a hundred and fifty miles away. The congregations were spiritually weak, and had been distracted by theological arguments. The first pastor in Anglesey, Seth Morris, had been a godly man, enjoying God's favour, but a Thomas Morris had come to the island, sown division, tried to take the pastorate himself, and finally had fallen into disgrace. It was *after* this time of misery (which Christmas Evans himself describes as "frost in May," producing universal blight) that the new minister from Llŷn arrived. The state of religion could be described as chaos.

One of the first things Christmas Evans did was to appoint a day for fasting and prayer in each of the preaching places and soon he had the pleasure of seeing God's work begin to prosper. "After that meeting," he observed, "it pleased the Lord to bless us – to increase our hearers, and to bring many to Christ."

He divided the island into four districts so that by preaching at three places each Sabbath, each gathering might have at least one Sabbath service a month. A map of Anglesey will reveal the extent of his labours, regularly visiting Llanfachreth, Amlwch, Holyhead, Capel Gwyn, Capel Newydd, Llanfair, Llanerchymedd, Llanddona, Beaumaris and Pencarneddi. During the week he untiringly visited the people at these great distances, attending to church affairs and exploring the possibility of building chapels. It was his great delight when the Lord Himself shone into his own heart.

As is normally the case, great was the enmity that was caused by the success of the gospel. One rumour that began to circulate was that Christmas Evans was paid half a crown for each person he baptized. This falsehood he squashed in his inimitable way. The opportunity came when he was to baptize the wife of a farmer of some social standing. A large crowd had gathered for the occasion. Lifting up his voice the preacher exclaimed, "They say I receive half a crown for each person I baptize. That is not true. I receive a crown – not half a one. They shall be my crown of joy and rejoicing in the great day." But unkind rumours, scattered abroad by the enemies of the truth, continued for many years.

What of his new home? Chapel and cottage stood together on a bleak, exposed piece of ground. But the minister's cottage was more like a poor shack; it seems almost impossible that anyone could have lived there. The stable for the horse or pony was part of the cottage. The furniture was poor and scanty. The bed was hardly suitable to sleep in; some of the boards had given way and it was supported by a few stone slabs. The door had rotted away. The roof was so low that the minister had to be careful whenever he stood up. The one poor room had to serve as living room, study, everything.

But here Christmas and his wife, Catherine, were happy. They proved that "godliness with contentment is great gain." "Having food and raiment," they were

BEAUMARIS CASTLE, ANGLESEY

content. He grew in the love and honour of the people, his preaching was blessed, his name was soon to become a household word throughout Wales, whilst Catherine proved a loving, helpful partner to him. Because of his poverty, which at this time was extreme, he would occasionally print a small pamphlet, which he sold in order to get a few extra pounds for necessary expenses.

In this little cottage he not only meditated and prayed but (amazing thing!) gained for himself a good knowledge of both Hebrew and Greek. Also he read deeply in Dr. Owen and Dr. Gill – his favourite authors; so we stand in no doubt of his theology. Much of Dr. Gill's commentary he translated into Welsh. (It was to the famous Robert Hall he once made the observation of how sad he was that Gill's works were not written in Welsh – which drew forth a sarcastic comment from the well-known preacher, who was of a different complexion.) But here, especially, he read the Word, and meditated, and prayed, sometimes cutting peculiar marks on his chair with a penknife while his thoughts were on things above. (In later years the venerable old chair was shown, almost with reverence, to visitors.)

And here he dreamed – by night and by day. One of his remarkable dreams he has recorded for us:

"I found myself at the gate of hell and, standing at the threshold, I saw an opening, beneath which was a vast sea of fire in wave-like motion. Looking at it, I said, 'What infinite virtue there must have been in the blood of Christ to have quenched, for His people, these awful flames!' Overcome with the feeling, I knelt down by the walls of hell, saying, 'Thanks be unto Thee, O great and blessed Saviour, that Thou has dried up this terrible sea of fire!' Whereupon Christ addressed me: 'Come this way, and I will show you how it was done.' Looking back, I beheld that the whole sea had disappeared. Jesus passed over the place, and said: 'Come, follow Me.'

"By this time, I was within what I thought were the gates of hell, where there were many cells, out of which it was impossible to escape. I found myself within one of these, and anxious to make my way out. Still I felt wonderfully calm as I had only just been conversing with Jesus, and because He had gone before me, although I had now lost sight of Him.

"I got hold of something, with which I struck the corner of the place in which I stood, saying, 'In the name of Jesus, open!' and it instantly gave way; so I did with all the enclosures, until I made my way out into the open field. Whom should I see there but brethren, none of whom, however, I knew, except a good old deacon, and their work was to attend to a nursery of trees; I joined them, and laid hold of a tree, saying, 'In the name of Jesus, be thou plucked up by the root!' And it came up as if it had been a rush. Hence I went forth, as I fancied, to work miracles,

43

saying, 'Now I know how the apostles wrought miracles in the name of Christ!'"

It is said that when meditating on his sermons, Christmas Evans was oblivious to all around. The story is told of two young ministers calling at Cildwrn cottage. They find the little table set for tea, but a man sitting there, Bible in hand, withdrawn from everything around. He takes no notice whatsoever of the visitors. To and fro he moves in his chair. He closes and opens his eyes; his face is dark and clouded. His wife nudges him to pass the empty cup to be filled; unconscious of what she is saying, he hands her his Bible. Still his face is dark. He rises, turns over page after page of Dr. Owen, tries another Puritan – but in vain. At length he throws himself on his knees in prayer; then rises, looks in his Bible again. His face grows calmer and brighter, the expression of agony disappears, and soon he comes forth from the conflict, welcomes his visitors, and talks with them kindly and lovingly.

CHAPTER 9

The One-Eyed Preacher of Wales

The great day in religious life in Wales in a past generation was the annual Association meetings of the Calvinistic Methodists or the Calvinistic Baptists. This has been described as "a kind of sacred Eisteddfod." On these occasions the best-known preachers were engaged to preach and up to fifteen thousand (some have thought twenty or even twenty-five thousand) people would gather together in the open air to hear them. It was as in ancient Israel when the tribes of the Lord went up to Jerusalem to worship. The farm labourers would be given time off, and farmers from a distance would travel by pony and trap.

Many are the stories told of these great Association meetings. For instance the following (similar to what is told of a Scottish communion). On one occasion the expected minister had not arrived so the farmer at whose home he was staying sent one of his servants to find out what was amiss. Approaching his

AN ASSOCIATION MEETING 1820
By kind permission of the National Library of Wales

room she could hear him exclaiming, "I will not go unless thou dost come with me!" Hurrying back to the scene of the meetings she explained what had happened: he was in conversation with someone and she wondered if he would not come. "Ah!" said her godly master, "he will come, and the other will come too." And, so the story goes, he did come, and his blessed Companion with him, and that night proved to be a very sacred meeting. This was the spirit of ministers and hearers in the best days of the Association meetings – not so much feeling certain the Lord *would* be with them as trembling to go in their own strength.

The story of Christmas Evans continues with one of these Association meetings in the year 1794, at Felinfoel near Llanelly, where he had gone as a hearer during the early years of his Anglesey ministry. But something had gone wrong. A vast concourse of people was assembled but, for some reason, there was no preacher. One can imagine the embarrassment.

Various ministers present were approached but all declined – no doubt shrinking from standing up before thousands at a moment's notice. In despair, Christmas Evans's old pastor, Timothy Thomas, was appealed to. He too declined – but added abruptly, "Ask that one-eyed lad from the north! I hear that he preaches wonderfully." So Christmas Evans was asked – as a last resort – and consented.

The vast congregation was filled with amazement, bordering on disgust, to see this tall, bony, haggard young man, uncouth and ill-dressed, ascend the platform. "Surely," they said, "that fellow has not been asked to preach!" (Despite his successful preaching tour from Llŷn he was still generally unknown.) They felt there was some mistake somewhere. But Christmas

47

Evans did preach.

Some of the congregation took the opportunity to wander away for refreshments. Others went to sit down and rest beneath the neighbouring hedges until one or more of the eminent speakers should arrive. Those who stayed hoped it would be short.

But the Holy Spirit was powerfully working in the heart of the young preacher. He stood up and announced for his text that wonderful scripture: "And you, that were sometime alienated and enemies in your mind by wicked works, yet now hath He reconciled, in the body of His flesh, through death, to present you holy, and unblameable, and unreproveable in His sight" (Colossians 1. 21, 22). His subject was the great theme of the gospel – man's ruin and separation from a holy God through sin, and the way of recovery through the atoning work of Christ at Calvary.

At first people felt their fears were justified; his manner was stiff and awkward. But then, eloquently, he began to warm to his theme. The Lord was with him. Closer and closer the people began to creep. Those who had wandered away began to return. The crowd grew more and more dense with eager listeners. The well-known preachers present listened, amazed at the preaching of this young man. Here and there the question was whispered, "Who is he?" Deeply affected by the discourse the multitude began to weep (and rejoice) and the words *"Gogoniant!"* (Glory!) and *"Bendigedig!"* (Blessed!) could be heard. Drawn from all parts of Wales, when at length the hearers wended their way homeward, they carried with them lasting memories of the sermon of "the one-eyed preacher."

No doubt there was much natural excitement in all this. At that time a great preacher in Wales was almost like some famous politician or sporting figure today, and the Association meetings like Parliament or Wembley. There was little or no entertainment in late eighteenth-century Wales. The pulpit was the stage, the platform, the orchestra, everything. In fact, until a hundred years ago, the pulpit in Wales was the only means of popular excitement or entertainment and, to a large extent, instruction. So it is not surprising that from that moment Christmas Evans was a famous man. Yet amidst it all there was something far deeper, far greater – a man of God, divinely raised up, filled with the Holy Spirit, and preaching in the fulness of the blessing of the gospel of Christ.

Christmas Evans always considered himself to be in the succession of such men as Daniel Rowlands and Howell Harris, "the children of the rising sun," as he called them. His prayer on one occasion was: "As Thou hast prospered Harris, Rowlands, Whitefield, Bunyan and Vavasor Powell, O prosper me!"*

*Strangely, there are many inconsistencies in the various lives of Christmas Evans. One reputable writer does, in fact, state that he was engaged to speak on this occasion! Yet all agree that from this time the name of Christmas Evans became a household word in Wales.

CHAPTER 10

Sandemanianism

It was during the earlier years of Christmas Evans's ministry in Anglesey (1794–1795) that the churches were shaken by what was known as the Sandemanian controversy – especially the Calvinistic Baptist churches, but others as well; and not only in Anglesey but throughout Wales. The Sandemanians took their name from a minister in Scotland, Robert Sandeman. Their great fault was a false view of faith; they counted it as a mere belief that the Bible is true, that Jesus is the Son of God, that He lived, died and rose again. They omitted the vital point: faith is personal trust in the Lord Jesus, so affecting the whole of the believer's life. The Sandemanians were clear on most Christian doctrines, but their teachings had a freezing, deadening effect on all who embraced them. In addition the Sandemanians became very harsh, bitter and even cynical. The reason for the remarkable spread of their influence in Wales was the preaching and personality of a remarkable man, John Richard Jones of Ramoth, near Harlech.

Sadly, for a time, Christmas Evans himself fell under this influence. In a letter written to M'Lean, the leading Sandemanian in Scotland, on November 28th, 1796, he makes it clear that he and his friends were remorselessly following all the peculiar Sandemanian practices, such as the kiss of charity, the feast of love, and washing of one another's feet. The sad thing is that *these were made conditions of soundness in the faith.*

In retrospect he wrote:

"The poison penetrated four counties: Anglesey, Carnarvon, Merioneth and Denbigh.

"Its first effect was to send away the hearers of the gospel; for this it prepared the way by alleging that the mass of hearers were 'of Babylon.' I lost in Anglesey almost all my old hearers; many of them attended the ministry with other denominations, and became united with them. There they had rest from the new condemning spirit among us.

"We thus almost entirely took down what had taken fifteen years to raise, and became again a despised people.

"Much distraction in the churches followed; a spirit of infallibility and worldly wisdom fell upon the people and on many of the preachers, until the weakest felt himself qualified to govern the church and the world."

After a time Christmas Evans felt that he had lost much of his zeal, earnestness and confidence. He realised something was wrong; he had lost something exceedingly precious, but he scarcely knew what. Conscience accused him. He said, "I had been robbed, to a great degree, of the spirit of prayer, and of the spirit of preaching." Both the spiritual life of Christmas Evans and his usefulness as a preacher were being affected.

It was largely through the blessing of God resting on the witness of one man, Thomas Jones of Glynceiriog, in Denbighshire, that the chilling influence of Sandemanianism was broken. But the Lord Himself powerfully broke the snare with Christmas Evans personally as he was travelling by himself up a lonely mountain road near Cader Idris. (Interestingly, it must have been about this time that Mary Jones walked barefoot over Cader Idris in hopes of purchasing a Welsh Bible at Bala.) He recounts his deliverance, almost dramatically:

> "I was weary," he says, referring to this period, "of a cold heart towards Christ, and His sacrifice, and the work of His Spirit – of a cold heart in the pulpit, in secret prayer, and in the study. For fifteen years previously, I had felt my heart burning within, as if going to Emmaus with Jesus. On a day ever to be remembered by me, as I was going from Dolgellau to Machynlleth, and climbing up towards Cader Idris, I considered it to be incumbent upon me to pray, however hard I felt in my heart, and however wordly the frame of my spirit was.
>
> "Having begun in the name of Jesus, I soon felt, as it were, the fetters loosening, and the old hardness of heart softening, and, as I thought, mountains of frost and snow dissolving and melting within me. This engendered confidence in my soul in the promise of the Holy Ghost. I felt my whole mind relieved from some great bondage; tears flowed copiously, and I was constrained to cry out for the gracious visits of God, by restoring to my soul the joys of His salvation; and that He would visit the churches in Anglesey that were under my care. I embraced in my supplications all the churches of the saints, and nearly all the ministers in the principality by their names.
>
> "This struggle lasted for three hours; it rose again and

again like one wave after another, or a high flowing tide driven by a strong wind, until my nature became faint by weeping and crying. Thus I resigned myself to Christ, body and soul, gifts and labours – all my life – every day and every hour that remained for me; and all my cares I committed to Christ. The road was mountainous and lonely, and I was wholly alone, and suffered no interruption in my wrestlings with God.

CADER IDRIS

"From this time, I was made to expect the goodness of God to the churches and to myself. Thus the Lord delivered me and the people of Anglesey from being carried away by the flood of Sandemanianism.

"In the first religious meetings after this, I felt as if I had been removed from the cold and sterile regions of spiritual frost into the verdant fields of divine promises. The former striving with God in prayer, and the longing anxiety for the conversion of sinners, which I had experienced at Llŷn, were now restored. I had a hold of the promises of God. The result was, when I returned home, the first thing that arrested my attention was that the Spirit was working also in the brethren in Anglesey, inducing in them a spirit of prayer, especially in two of the deacons, who were particularly importunate that God would visit us in mercy, and render the Word of His grace effectual amongst us for the conversion of sinners."

From about this time, also, belongs a remarkable "solemn covenant with God" which he made and signed. (It is interesting how many eminently godly men in the past did this!) It was written, he says, "under a deep sense of the evil of my own heart, and in dependence upon the infinite grace and merit of the Redeemer." Altogether there are thirteen clauses, each personally signed: "C.E." Among them are:

"IV. I entreat Thee, Jesus, the Son of God, in power grant me, for the sake of Thy agonizing death, a covenant interest in Thy blood, which cleanseth; in Thy righteousness, which justifieth; and in Thy redemption, which delivereth. I entreat an interest in Thy blood, for Thy *blood's* sake, and a part in Thee, for Thy name's sake, which Thou hast given among men. Amen.

"VII. I give myself in a particular manner to Thee, O Jesus Christ the Saviour, to be preserved from the falls into which many stumble, that Thy name (in Thy cause) may not be blasphemed or wounded, that my peace may not be injured, that Thy people may not be grieved, and that Thine enemies may not be hardened. Amen.

"IX. Search me now, and lead me into plain paths of judgment. Let me discover in this life what I am before Thee, that I may not find myself of another character when I am shown in the light of the immortal world, and open my eyes in all the brightness of eternity. Wash me in Thy redeeming blood. Amen.

"XI. Grant, O Jesus, and take upon Thyself the preparing of me for death, for Thou art God; there is no need but for

Thee to speak the word. If possible (Thy will be done), leave me not long in affliction, nor to die suddenly without bidding adieu to my brethren, and let me die in their sight after a short illness. Let all things be ordered against the day of removing from one world to another, that there be no confusion nor disorder but a quiet discharge in peace. O grant me this, for the sake of Thine agony in the garden. Amen.

"XII. Grant, O blessed Lord, that nothing may grow and be matured in me to occasion Thee to cast me off from the service of the sanctuary, like the sons of Eli; and for the sake of Thine unbounded merit, let not my days be longer than my usefulness. O let me not be like lumber in a house in the end of my days, in the way of others to work. Amen."

His own comment is as follows:

"After forming this covenant I felt great calmness and perfect peace. I had the feelings of a poor man who has just come under the protection of the royal family, and has obtained an annual pension for life, the dreadful fear of poverty and want having left his house for ever. This is what it is to abide under the shadow of the Almighty, and to hide under His wings until all dangers are past."

Now, strengthened in a special way by the Lord, he preached with renewed energy and zeal, and special blessings rested on his labours in the following years. Naturally speaking these were dark days in Anglesey as in so many places (the ending of the Napoleonic Wars). The price of wheat was so high that bread was a luxury; fish was the only food that was plentiful. Poor children were starving and disease was rampant. Yet in two years (1814 and 1815) 600, professing to be called by God's grace, were added to the church under his immediate care, while his ten preaching places increased to twenty. "The wilderness now blossomed as a rose," he wrote, "and in the desolate places was heard the voice of song."

Yet the years of controversy were not entirely without good. Preaching, generally, had degenerated in North Wales, much being from curious texts and with strange spiritualisation. After the dreadful storm, it was observed that preaching became much more sober in handling God's Word, seeking more for a gracious experimental effect and the purifying of the heart. So a leading Welsh minister had to testify "Out of the eater came forth meat, and out of the strong came forth sweetness."

CHAPTER 11

The Graveyard Sermon

It was probably to this time that his famous "graveyard sermon" belonged, a sermon that became extensively known, even outside Wales. It is interesting that when in 1909 a seven-volume work entitled *The World's Great Sermons* appeared, this sermon of Christmas Evans was included – apparently the only one by a Welsh preacher, and one of the few by a Baptist.

It appears to have been first preached in a small dell among the Carnarvonshire mountains. It was summer; the grass still green; brooks rippling round; the spot hemmed in by jagged crags and the cliffs of tall mountains.

There was a preliminary service: verses of a hymn, in the beautiful minor key so typical of Welsh tunes, sung by thousands of tongues; reading; prayer; singing again; then a short sermon.

Then Christmas Evans appears. He is described at this period of his life as almost six feet high; of robust, athletic frame; his black hair thick, coarse, not very well arranged; dark, arched and heavy eyebrows; a ponderous, awkward bearing still, with that one eye which the famous Robert Hall said was so brilliant that "it could have lighted an army through a forest on a dark night." He stands there, very calm and quiet, but his face very expressive. He gives out a verse or two of a well-known Welsh hymn and, while it is being sung, takes out a small phial from his waistcoat pocket. It is laudanum; and wetting the tips of his fingers he draws them over his blind eye to deaden the excruciating pain which sometimes, on such occasions, possessed him. (Occasionally, snuff, which he carried in his waistcoat pocket, helped him.)

Then he announces the text, Romans, chapter 5, verse 15: "If through the offence of one many be dead, much more the grace of God, and the gift by grace, which is by one Man, Jesus Christ, hath abounded unto many."

First of all he speaks of the universal total depravity and sinfulness of men. *Tekel* is written on every heart. Solemnly he opens up man's lost and ruined condition and, as he does, the people draw nearer. Some rise from their seats. Some begin to weep. An old godly clergyman, despised and hated for the truth's sake, rejoices to hear the old, loved truths set forth, and weeps profusely.

Then he begins to speak of the whole world as a graveyard.

"Methinks," exclaimed the impassioned preacher, "I find myself standing upon the summit of one of the highest of the everlasting hills, permitted from thence to take a survey of the whole earth; and all before me I see a wide and far-spread burial-ground, a graveyard, over which lie scattered the countless multitudes of the wretched and perishing children of Adam! The ground is full of hollows, the yawning caverns of death; and over the whole scene broods a thick cloud of darkness. No light from above shines upon it, there is no ray of sun or moon, there is no beam, even of a little candle, seen through all its borders. It is walled all around, but it has gates, large and massive, ten thousand times stronger than all the gates of brass forged among men. They are one and all safely locked – the hand of divine Law has locked them; and so firmly secured are the strong bolts that all the created powers even of the heavenly world, were they to labour to all eternity, could not drive so much as one of them back. How hopeless is the wretchedness to which the race is doomed! Into what irrecoverable depths of ruin has sin plunged the people who sit there in darkness and in the shadow of death, while there by the brazen gates stands the inflexible guard, brandishing the flaming sword of undeviating Law!

"But see! In the cool of the day, there is one descending from the eternal hills in the distance. It is Mercy! the radiant form of Mercy, seated in the chariot of Divine Promise. She comes through the worlds of the universe. She pauses here to mark the imprisoned and grave-like aspect of our once fair world. Her eye affected her heart as she beheld the misery, and heard the cry of despair, borne upon the four winds of heaven. She could not pass by, nor pass on. She wept over the melancholy scene, and she said, 'Oh that I might enter! I would bind up their wounds, I would relieve their sorrows, I would save their souls!'

"An embassy of angels, commissioned from heaven to some other world, paused at the sight; and heaven forgave that pause. They saw Mercy standing by the gate, and they cried, 'Mercy, canst thou not enter? Canst thou look upon that world and not pity? Canst thou pity and not relieve?' And Mercy, in tears, replied, 'I can see, and I can pity, but I cannot relieve.' 'Why dost thou not enter?' inquired the heavenly host. 'Oh,' said Mercy, 'Law has barred the gate against me, and I must not, and I cannot unbar it.' And Law stood there watching the gate, and the angels asked of him, 'Why wilt thou not suffer Mercy to enter?' And he said, 'No one can enter here and live'; and the thunder of his voice outspoke the wailings within.

"Then again I heard Mercy cry, 'Is there no entrance for me into this field of death? May I not visit these caverns of the grave and seek, if it may be, to raise some at least of these children of destruction, and bring them to the light of day? Open, Justice, open! drive back these iron bolts, and let me in that I may proclaim the jubilee of redemption to the children of the dust!' And then I heard Justice reply, 'Mercy! surely thou lovest Justice too well to wish to burst these gates by force of arm, and thus to obtain entrance by lawless violence. I cannot open the door. I am not angry with these unhappy ones, I have no delight in their death or in hearing their cries as they lie upon the burning hearth of the great fire, kindled by the wrath of God, in the land that is lower than the grave. *But without shedding of blood there is no remission.*'

"So Mercy expanded her wings, splendid beyond the brightness of the morning when its rays are seen shooting over mountains of pearl – and Mercy renewed her flight amongst the unfallen worlds. She re-ascended into the mid air but could not proceed far because she could not forget the sad sight of the Graveyard-World, the melancholy prison. She returned to her native throne in the heaven of heavens; it was a glorious high throne, unshaken and untarnished by the fallen fate of men and angels. Even there she could not forget what she had witnessed and wept over, and she weighed the woes of the sad world against the doom of eternal Law. She could not forget the prison and the graveyard, and she re-descended with a more rapid and radiant flight, and she stood again by the gate, but again was denied admission. And the two stood there together, Justice and Mercy; and Justice dropped his brandishing sword while they held converse together. And while they talked, there was silence in heaven.

"' Is there then no admission on any terms whatever?' she said. 'Ah, yes,' said Justice; 'but then they are terms which no created being can fulfil. I demand atoning death for the eternal life of those who lie in this graveyard; I demand divine life for their ransom.' And while they were talking, behold there stood by them a third Form, fairer than the children of men, radiant with the glory of heaven. He cast a look upon the graveyard. And He said to Mercy, 'Accept the terms.' 'Where is the security?' said Justice. 'Here,' said Mercy, pointing to the radiant Stranger, 'is my bond. Four thousand years from hence, demand its payment on Calvary. To redeem men,' said Mercy, 'I will be incarnate in the Son of God; the Lamb will be slain for the life of this Graveyard World.'

"The bond was accepted, and Mercy entered the graveyard leaning on the arm of Justice. She spoke to the prisoners. Centuries rolled by. So went on the gathering of the firstfruits in the field of redemption. Still ages passed away, and at last the clock of prophecy struck the fulness of time. The bond, which had been committed to patriarchs and prophets, had to be redeemed; a long series of rites and ceremonies, sacrifices and oblations, had been instituted to perpetuate the memory of that solemn deed.

"At the close of the four thousandth year, when Daniel's seventy weeks were accomplished, Justice and Mercy appeared on the hill of Calvary. Angels and archangels, cherubim and seraphim, principalities and powers, left their thrones and mansions of glory, and bent over the battlements of heaven, gazing in mute amazement and breathless suspense upon the solemn scene. At the foot of Calvary's hill was beheld the Son of God. 'Lo, I come,' He said; 'in the bond it is written of Me.' He appeared without the gates of Jerusalem, crowned with thorns, and followed by the weeping church. It was with Him the hour and the power of darkness. Above Him were all the vials of divine wrath, and the thunders of the eternal Law. Round Him were all the powers of darkness. The monsters of the pit, huge, fierce and relentless, were there: the lions as a great army, gnashing their teeth ready to tear Him in pieces; the unicorns, a countless host, were rushing onwards to thrust Him through; and there were the bulls of Bashan roaring terribly; the dragons of the pit unfolding themselves, and shooting out their stings; and dogs, many, all round the mountain.

FIELD PREACHING, ANGLESEY

"And He passed through this dense array, an unresisting Victim led as a lamb to the slaughter. He took the bond from the hand of Justice and, as He was nailed to the cross, He nailed it to the cross; and all the hosts of hell, though invisible to man, had formed a ring around it. The rocks rent, the sun shrank from the scene, as Justice lifted his right hand to the throne, exclaiming, 'Fire of heaven, descend and consume this Sacrifice!' The fires of heaven, animated with living spirit, answered the call, 'We come! we come! and, when we have consumed that Victim, we will burn the world.' They burst, blazed, devoured. The blood of the Victim was fast dropping. The hosts of hell were shouting, until the humanity of Emmanuel gave up the ghost. The fire went on burning until the ninth hour of the day, but when it touched the Deity of the Son of God, it expired. Justice dropped the fiery sword at the foot of the cross; and the Law joined with the prophets in witnessing to the righteousness which is by faith in the Son of God, for all had heard the dying Redeemer exclaim, 'It is finished!'

"The weeping church heard it, and lifting up her head cried too, 'It is finished!' Attending angels hovering near heard it and, winging their flight, they sang, 'It is finished!' The powers of darkness heard the acclamations of the universe, and hurried away from the scene in death-like feebleness. He triumphed over them openly. The graves of the old burial ground have been thrown open, and gales of life have blown over the valley of dry bones, and an exceeding great army has already been sealed to our God as among the living in Zion; for so the bond was paid and eternal redemption secured."

This was certainly remarkable preaching. Someone wrote: "All the stores of his energy, and the resources of his voice, which was one of great compass, depth and sweetness, seemed reserved for the closing portion of the picture, when he represented the routed and battered hosts of evil retreating from the cross, where they anticipated a triumph, and met a signal and irretrievable overthrow."

Christmas Evans's great theme was the atonement.

It was the old theology: the curse of a broken law; the substitutionary death of the Son of God, bearing the curse for His people; the complete removing of the curse, and every blessing flowing to sinners through the blood of Christ.

How many of the old Welsh hymns from that period echo the same sentiments! For instance, the following hymn, written by his contemporary, the renowned preacher John Elias (1774–1841):

> "And was it for my sin
>   That Jesus suffered so,
> When moved by His all-powerful love
>   He came to earth below?
>
> "Thy holy law fulfilled,
>   Atonement now is made,
> And our great debt, too great for us,
>   He now has fully paid.
>
> "He suffered pain and death,
>   When on the hill brought low;
> His blood will wash the guilty clean,
>   As pure and white as snow.
>
> "For in His death our death
>   Died with Him on the tree,
> And a great number by His blood
>   Will go to heaven made free.
>
> "When Jesus bowed His head
>   And, dying, took our place,
> The veil was rent, a way was found
>   To that pure home of grace.
>
> "He conquered blackest hell;
>   He trod the serpent down;
> A host from fetters He'll set free
>   By grace to be God's own."

CHAPTER 12

In Labours Oft

As a result of God's blessing resting upon his ministry in Anglesey Christmas Evans's influence among the churches became very great. He was a pastor of pastors, in fact a "bishop" in the modern sense of the word. And his labours were incessant. There were the societies under his care, the meeting houses to be built, the funds to be found, the cases of discipline to be dealt with, the pastors to be set apart to work with him. Most of the ministers were men still in business, with their own domestic affairs, and needing much help and guidance from their better-known and esteemed colleague.

In all the various gatherings he was automatically the president. And some of the meetings were very primitive, as well they might be in this raw state of society. There was no "Mr. Evans"; he was "Christmas Evans" to his face and behind his back. Yet with all this, affectionate familiarity did not give way to lack of respect. Christmas Evans was able to hold his post as moderator with dignity without losing the love of the brethren. Order was maintained with a "William, you have spoken before. Be done;" or "Richard, you have forgotten the question before the meeting. Be silent." In fact a visiting minister from South Wales, who wished to impress by his eloquence, was silenced with "Sit down, David, sit down."

The meetings of the Association in Anglesey were times of great joy and encouragement to him. Great was his concern that in no way the Lord's holy name might be dishonoured. Religious politicians on the island were very jealous of each other and the poor Baptists were suspected of being disloyal to the crown, even called "Jacobins"! It is said that so concerned was Christmas Evans lest any fuel should be added to inflame this groundless rumour that he would kneel on the platform near to the minister who opened the Association in prayer, and remind him if he omitted to pray for the king (George III) and the royal family!

So the name of Calvinistic Baptist became respected and esteemed in North Wales.

He was also at times involved in controversy. When the practice of believers' baptism was assailed in a book by Peter Williams of Wern, which caused a great stir in Wales, he answered in a book with the strange title *Sarah and her Son Casting out the Bondmaid and her Son!* Also he wrote very strongly on the doctrine of Particular Redemption (1811), this being necessitated by the inroads of the Wesleyans into North Wales. Later he published a book *Redemption within the Circle of Election.* In a letter to a Welsh magazine he thus epitomized his own theology: "The reader will find all my views in the Epistles of Paul and in Dr.

Owen's *Death of Death"* (the classic defence of particular redemption).

He was never rich; £30 a year (57½p a week!) was the *most* he ever received till leaving Anglesey. Yet the record is that "he was given to hospitality," amazingly so, many passers by staying at his house, while he constantly contributed his sovereign or half sovereign to some worthy cause. If presented with a new suit, he would often give it away. Truly it can be said of him: "As poor, yet making many rich; as having nothing, and yet possessing all things."

His wife Catherine was a wonderful help. Of her spiritual outlook her husband wrote that she had "a deep sense of corruption, and of the utter impossibility of her salvation by the deeds of the law, and the indispensable necessity, in order to acceptance before God, of the merits of Christ and their imputation to the soul through faith in His righteousness. She had very elevated views of the sacrifice of Christ, which was her rock and strong tower." It appears that she was rich in faith and possessed a calm, quiet, practical mind. Hers was often a lonely life in the solitary cottage – no hint of luxury intruding and her husband often away.

It seems a strange feature of the Welsh chapels of the time that though they so dearly loved sermons and almost idolised preachers, yet they did little to help with the daily comforts of their ministers. For the most part Christmas Evans was content with his life of poverty though it is recorded that on one occasion his soul was filled with righteous indignation. After the hearers had spoken of the wonderful sermon, he was informed he would be recompensed at the resurrection of the just! "Yes, yes, no doubt of that," was the reply. "But I have to live till I get there. And what of my poor old white horse? That needs to be fed now. For my horse there will be no resurrection!"

But all this worked for good. Wales never possessed a more unselfish or humbler Christian. His one concern was for the honour and glory of God. About his own personal appearance he was unconcerned. It is, in fact, recorded that on one occasion Catherine had, with some difficulty, succeeded in supplying her husband with a new hat. Travelling to preach soon afterwards, his horse needed water and, coming to a brook, he was at loss for a bucket. What could be done? The only thing seemed to be to use the new hat! It is no wonder that on his return home Catherine was amazed at its worsened condition. On another occasion he returned home without his best coat, having given it to an Irish tramp.

Yet with all this there was no loss of dignity; he possessed the true dignity which the grace of God gives. He had a "presence." Nearly six foot tall, finely proportioned, his whole bearing was dignified and majestic, and did not depend on outward adornment. One who knew him well applied to him the words of the psalm: "All thy garments smell of myrrh, and aloes, and cassia," the sweet savour of Christ.

He was a man of prayer. We read of his being in earnest prayer throughout the whole of a ten-mile journey. For many years he was accustomed to retire for prayer three times a day, and also to rise for prayer at midnight. He wrestled with God in prayer both for his subject in preaching and for God's blessing to attend. He prayed his way through trials – and out of them. He prayed even for his enemies in their trials; in an eminent degree he possessed a forgiving spirit. And he knew what answers to prayer were. So he was a "wrestling Jacob." He writes:

> "Christ, according to the riches of His grace, gave me a
> fresh spirit of prayer, with a special enjoyment of His
> presence, until I became a prince in the confidence that
> the Lord Jesus was in alliance with me, as Jacob felt
> before he went to meet his brother Esau, whose anger he
> greatly feared. No Esau succeeded against me, though he
> might come with four hundred armed men."

His whole life in Anglesey was plagued by chapel
debts. Chapels rose – it had to be so as people in
scattered villages thronged to hear the Word.
Hundreds were brought into church fellowship.
Chapels that had been built had to be enlarged. And on
Christmas Evans the whole burden of the cost seems to
have fallen. He had no money; but he was well-known,
eloquent, popular. So "Christmas Evans" was the
name on which the money was lent. But then the
interest was due, or the debt had to be paid. What then?
He must go forth to the south of Wales and beg money
from the richer churches.

This is why year after year there were those long,
lonely journeys on his horse through wild regions
where sometimes he met not even a solitary traveller
throughout the day. "Jack," he would say to his faithful
horse, "we have only to cross one low mountain, and
there will be oats, water and a warm stable," and Jack
would neigh his appreciation. For many years he went
twice annually to the south: once to the vast
Association meeting, wherever it may be, and once (in
winter) on his "begging tour." Occasionally Catherine
accompanied him, and he would be away weeks at a
time.

We pause to think for a moment of these journeys:

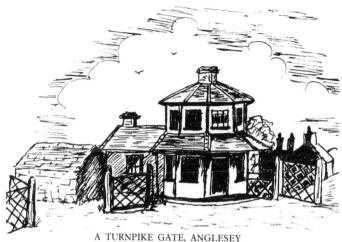

A TURNPIKE GATE, ANGLESEY

through mountain villages; past ruined castles and monasteries, now turned into barns; through wild and beautiful scenes, narrow glens where mountain torrents roared. Often these journeys were through storm and rain, sometimes far into the night. Uncomplainingly he went on, for he loved his Master and his work. And the Lord was with him: sometimes reviving frozen churches; sometimes planting new ones; sometimes commencing new preaching stations.

Travelling on horseback he was able to read, and even more to meditate, and he owed much to the good sense of his beloved horse that he seldom lost his way, and was never late. Just one instance is mentioned when his horse, feeling thirsty, wandered off the road into a nearby river or pond to drink, and Christmas Evans was awakened from his meditations to find the water almost up to the tops of his boots.

During these journeys he studied hard so that he might be able to preach in English. He had been able to

70

read some of the English divines while still in Llŷn, but it was not till he was thirty-three that he began to grapple with English grammar. "My English was very broken," he says, "and yet it was my ardent wish to be able to preach in it. I made it a matter of prayer, as I never succeeded in anything without doing so. This the Lord in time enabled me to do. I was about forty years of age when I learned to read my Hebrew Bible and Greek Testament."

In the homes of the people he was happy with the poorest of food; his favourite porridge was all he wanted. And sometimes the conditions were very primitive. The "prophet's chamber" in one place was so flimsy that he woke one morning to find his feet protruding through the wall and almost hit by a passing cart.

It was in the houses of the poor that he was able to indulge in one of his hobbies – collecting recipes for medical treatment (either of men or horses). It is said that on some of his papers, along with remarks on some deep point of theology, might be found a recipe for the cure of asthma that he had picked up on his journeyings. Also he loved gathering specimens of herbs on his travels or, alternatively, showing his skill in sharpening razors or knives. There was nothing of "the great preacher" about him.

In this way he travelled from north to south some forty times. He always preached once each day of the week, twice on the Lord's day. Of course, vast congregations welcomed him but the collections were normally very small. And he had the indignity of having to stand at the door after sermon, hat in hand, to take his own collection.

On one occasion, though, he did have a good

collection. Preaching in a district notorious for sheep stealing, he spoke of this great evil, and at the end pleaded with the people: "If you have been guilty of sheep stealing, please do not put any money in the collection." Needless to say, not a person passed him that night without making some contribution!

There was frequently complaint from the ministers in the south that he came too often (begging), but only in this way were the chapels of Anglesey and North Wales built. The burden he carried was very heavy. He wrote:

> "I had only seventeen pounds a year for all my services. The other preachers were young and inexperienced, and the members threw all the responsibility on me, as children do upon a father. My anxiety often moved me in the depths of the night to cry out to God to preserve His cause from shame. God's promises to sustain His cause in the world greatly comforted me. I would search for the divine promises to this effect, and plead them in prayer, until I felt as confident as if every farthing had been paid."

Like the Apostle Paul he could speak of "the care of all the churches."

But what blessings did he know in his own soul as he went on his solitary journeys, alone yet not alone? And what blessings were there in the huge gatherings in some of those remote and lonely spots where, without a trace of humour, the announcement in winter would often be, "Mr. So-and-so will preach next Lord's day, *if he comes*"?

CHAPTER 13

The Bunyan of Wales

No doubt in God's mysterious purposes the chapel difficulties of Anglesey were overruled so that thousands throughout Wales might hear the glorious gospel preached. Some, in more recent times, have almost patronisingly spoken of Christmas Evans's "rugged, old-fashioned preaching." It was the whole counsel of God that he preached, especially emphasising man's ruin through the fall, his liability to divine wrath, and the wonderful provision Christ has made for His people at Calvary. The doctrines he preached were those commonly called Calvinism, but which really are the doctrines of the New Testament. "Preach the whole counsel of God," he wrote to a young minister, "from predestination to glorification."

Against the background of the many trials Christmas Evans had to endure, there was always the warm, loving reception he received at the great Association meeting. Here he was both honoured and loved. Admittedly there was much excitement, but who can imagine the longing expectation of many poor, simple villagers as they awaited the leading preacher, "their wonderful and well-loved prophet"? It is said that among his hearers at such meetings at times would be the renowned John Elias "with tearful eye and his whole form in motion."

One of these occasions has been graphically described:

"So, along all the roads, there presses an untiring crowd, showing that something unusual is going on somewhere. The roads are all picturesque and lively with all sorts of people, on foot, on horseback, in old farm carts, and even in carriages; all wending their way to the largest and most central chapel of the neighbourhood. It is the chief service. It is a Sabbath evening; the congregation is wedged together in the spacious house of God; it becomes almost insupportable, but the Welsh like it. The service has not commenced, and a cry is already raised that it had better be held in an adjoining field; but it is said this would be inconvenient. The doors, the windows, are all thrown open; and so the time goes on, and the hour for the commencement of the service arrives. All eyes are strained as the door opens beneath the pulpit, and the minister of the congregation comes in, and makes his way, as well as he can, for himself and his friend, the great preacher – there he is! that tall, commanding figure, that is he, the 'one-eyed man of Anglesey.'"

Christmas Evans's preaching was undoubtedly quaint and unusual, and certainly it would be wrong for any to imitate it. He was an orator, but tended to preach at times in allegories.

Witness his preaching on "Satan Walking in Dry Places":

74

"'There he is,' said Satan; 'his veins are full of blood, his bones are full of marrow. I will cast my sparks into his bosom, and set all his passions on fire; I will lead him on, and he shall rob his master, and lose his place, and find another, and rob again, and do worse; and he shall go on from worse to worse, and then his soul shall sink, never to rise again, into the lake of fire.' But just then, as he was about to dart a fiery temptation into the heart of the youth, the evil one heard him sing,

"'Guide me, O Thou great Jehovah,
    Pilgrim through this barren land;
I am weak, but Thou art mighty,
    Hold me by Thy powerful hand;
        Strong Deliverer,
Be Thou still my Strength and Shield.'

'Oh, but this is a dry place,' said the fiery dragon as he fled away.

"But I saw him pass on," said the preacher, "hovering, like a hawk or a vulture, in the air, and casting about for a suitable place where he might nestle his black wings; when, at the edge of the moor, he came to a lovely valley. The hills rose round it, it was a beautiful, still, meadow-like spot, watered by a lovely stream; and there, beneath the eaves of a little cottage, he saw a girl, some eighteen years of age, a flower among the flowers. She was knitting, or sewing, at the cottage door. Said Satan, 'She will do for me. I will whisper the evil thought in her heart, and she shall turn it over and over again until she learns to love it; and then the evil thought shall be an evil deed; and then she shall be obliged to leave her village, and go to the great town, and she shall live a life of evil, all astray from the paths of my Almighty Enemy. Oh, I will make her mine, and then, by-and-by, I will cast her over the precipices, and she shall sink, sink into the furnace of divine wrath.' And so he hastened to approach, and dart into the mind of the maiden. But while he was approaching, all the hills and crags seemed to break out into singing, as her sweet voice rose, high and clear, chanting out the words,

> "'Jesus, Lover of my soul,
>   Let me to Thy bosom fly,
> While the nearer waters roll,
>   While the tempest still is high.
> Other refuge have I none,
>   Hangs my helpless soul on Thee;
> Leave, ah, leave me not alone,
>   Still support, and comfort me.'

'This is a very dry place, too,' said the dragon, as he fled away.

"And so he passed from the valley among the hills, but with hot rage. 'I will have a place to dwell in!' he said. 'I will somehow leap over the fences and the hedges of the purpose, and covenant, and grace of God. I do not seem to have succeeded with the young, I will try the old'; for passing down the village street, he saw an old woman. She too was sitting at the door of her cot, and spinning on her little wheel. 'Ah!' said Satan, 'it will be good to lay hold of her grey hairs, and make her taste of the lake that burneth with fire and brimstone.' And he descended on the eaves of the cot; but as he approached near, he heard the trembling, quavering voice of the aged woman murmuring to herself lowlily, 'For the mountains shall depart, and the hills be removed, but My kindness shall not depart from thee, neither shall the covenant of My peace be removed, saith the Lord that hath mercy on thee.' And the words hurt the evil one, as well as disappointed him; they wounded him as he fled away, saying, 'Another dry place!'

"Ah, poor Devil!" exclaimed the preacher, "and he is usually so very successful! but he was quite unsuccessful that day. And now it was night, and he was scudding about, like a bird of prey, upon his black wings, and pouring forth his screams of rage. But he passed through another little Welsh village, the white cottages gleaming out in the white moonlight on the sloping hillside. And there was a cottage, and in the upper room there was a faint light trembling, and 'Oh,' said the Devil to himself, 'Devil, thou hast been a very foolish Devil today, and there, in that room, where the lamplight is, old Williams is slowly, surely wasting away. Over eighty, or I am mistaken; not much mind left; and he has borne the burden and heat of the day, as they call it. Thanks to me, he has had a hard time of it. He has had very few mercies to be thankful for; he has not found serving God, I think, a very profitable business. Come, cheer up, Devil, it will be a grand thing if thou canst get him to doubt a bit, and then to despair a bit, and then to curse God, and die. That will make up for this day's losses.'

"Then he entered the room. There was the old man lying on the poor bed, and his long, thin, wasted hands and fingers lying on the coverlid; his eyes closed, the long silvery hair falling over the pillow. Now, Satan, make haste, or it will be too late. The hour is coming, there is even a stir in every room in the house; they seem to know that the old man is passing. But as Satan himself moved before the bed to dart into the mind of the old man, the patriarch rose in bed, stretched forth his hands, and pinned his enemy to the wall as he exclaimed, 'Though I walk through the valley of the shadow of death, I will fear no evil: for Thou art with me, Thy rod and Thy staff they comfort me. Thou preparest a table before me, in *the presence of mine enemy*; Thou anointest my head with oil; my cup runneth over. Surely goodness and mercy shall follow me all the days of my life, and I shall dwell in the house of my God for ever.' Oh *that* was a fearfully dry place! The old man sank back; it was all over. Those words beat Satan down to the bottom of his own bottomless pit, glad to escape from such confusion and shame, and exclaiming, 'I will return to the place from

AN OLD WELSH SHEEP BRIDGE

whence I came, for this is too dry for me.'"

Certainly this could not be imitated. But it is wrong to think of Christmas Evans merely as quaint – unusual – dramatic. He was both a godly man and a great preacher. (We can form no real idea of his ministry: first, because black-and-white print is like a skeleton to the living man; and, second, because the sermons are translations from Welsh.) There is a solid foundation of deep doctrine and gracious experience, and Christ is truly exalted.

One of his best-known sermons was on the mad Gadarene: "Jesus said unto him, Go home unto thy friends, and tell them how great things the Lord hath done for thee, and hath had compassion on thee." The preacher seemed to revel in dramatic scenery and pictorial imagination.

First, he described the Gadarene as a castle, strongly armed, garrisoned with a legion of devils, but pictured an almighty Conqueror majestically sailing across the Sea of Galilee, bidding winds and waves obey Him.

Next he described the person of the Gadarene. His description, couched in Welsh imagery, is grotesque and gruesome, so that the congregation was almost in terror.

Then he spoke of the casting out of the demons and the herd of swine rushing headlong into the lake.

"One of them said, 'They are all gone!'"

"' No, sure not all gone into the sea!'"

"'Yes, every one of them, *the black hog* and all. They are all drowned!'"

Finally he imagines the now cleansed and restored sinner returning to his own house – people staring through the windows, his children running in and telling their mother: "We never saw father coming home as he comes today. He walks on the footpath, and turns round the corner of the fence. He used to come towards the house as straight as a line over fences, ditches and hedges." Then the Gadarene's wife is afraid to let him in the house.

Now surely there can be no excuse for all this.

But then the mad Gadarene's testimony when, at the end, he seeks to tell them who this wonderful Person, Jesus, is. We have seldom read anything more sacred:

"I am come to show you what great things God has done for me. He loved me with an everlasting love. He redeemed me from the curse of the law, and the threatenings of vindictive justice. He saved me from the power and dominion of sin. He cast the devils out of my heart, and made that heart, which was a den of thieves, the temple of the Holy Spirit. I cannot tell you how much I love my Saviour. Jesus Christ is the foundation of my hope, the object of my faith, and the centre of my affections. I can venture my immortal soul upon Him.

"He is my best Friend. He is altogether lovely – the Chief among ten thousand. He is my wisdom, righteousness, sanctification and redemption. There is enough in Him to make a poor sinner rich, and a miserable sinner happy. His flesh and blood is my food, His righteousness my wedding garment, and His blood is efficacious to cleanse me from all my sins. Through Him I can obtain eternal life; for He is the brightness of the Father's glory, and the express image of His Person: in whom dwelleth all the fulness of the Godhead bodily.

"He deserves my highest esteem, and my warmest gratitude. Unto Him who loved me with an eternal love, and washed me in His own blood, unto Him be the glory, dominion and power for ever and ever! For He has rescued my soul from hell. He plucked me as a brand from the burning. He took me out of the miry clay, and out of a horrible pit. He set my feet upon a rock, and established my goings, and put in my mouth a new song of praise, and glory to Him! Glory to Him for ever! Glory to God in the highest! Glory to God for ever and ever! Let the whole earth praise Him! Yea, let all the people praise Him!"

We are not surprised to learn that the place became a Bochim (the place of weeping); the hearers wept. Sobs, tears, prayers and praises mingled together. One present said that "the people seemed like the inhabitants of a city which had been shaken by an earthquake that, in their escape, rushed into the streets, falling upon the earth, calling upon God."

CHAPTER 14

The Waters of Marah

As Christmas Evans neared sixty years of age, his pathway became clouded.

His first sorrow was the loss of his beloved wife, Catherine, in 1823. A godly woman of deep and devout convictions, she was an eminently suitable wife for a minister. Their home had long been a place of self-denial and her husband used to tell "if there happened to be on our table one thing better than the other, she would modestly but cheerfully and earnestly resist all importunity to partake of it until she ascertained that there was enough for us both."

It seems incredible to read of all the good Catherine did. She constantly found food for needy people and poor children. Having no children of her own, she spent her time making clothes for the poor families at the chapel. Money and bread were given to thousands of Irish labourers who passed her door on their way to the English harvests, while a loving welcome awaited any travelling minister who passed that way. She never had the best of health but was invariably cheerful. Above all she was as a soothing balm to the oft-wounded and tormented spirit of her husband. She knew how to comfort, to help, to console.

One great struggle she had at the end of her life; she had been deeply wounded and hurt and found it very hard to forgive. She prayed, struggled, even agonized – till at last she felt she had been enabled to forgive.

Her last illness was long. For the last two years she was in much pain and weakness through a complication of disorders, but she was blessed with a spirit of submission. The last night of her life she repeated a beautiful Welsh hymn; then three times sighing, "Lord Jesus, have mercy upon me!" she breathed forth her soul into the arms of her Redeemer, and died in perfect peace.

There was sadness in Cildwrn cottage as Christmas was left alone with his griefs and burdens. Soon after his bereavement he was threatened with a legal prosecution on account of some chapel debts, for which he had to bear the responsibility. In his low state of mind he was deeply disturbed, especially because of the honour of the Saviour's name. However, he knew the worth of prayer. "They talk of casting me into a court of law," he said, "where I have never been, and hope I shall never go; but I will cast them first into the court of Jesus Christ."

At length he received the letter at a monthly meeting he attended. "On my return home," he wrote, "I had fellowship with God during the whole journey of ten miles and, arriving at my own house, I went upstairs to my own chamber and poured forth my heart before the Redeemer, who has in His hands all authority and power." The following was his prayer:

"O blessed Lord! in Thy merit I confide, and trust to be heard. Lord, some of my brethren have run wild; and forgetting their duty and obligations to their father in the gospel, they threaten me with the law of the land. Weaken, I beseech Thee, their designs in this, as Thou didst wither the arm of Jeroboam; and soften them, as Thou didst soften the mind of Esau and disarmed him of his warlike temper against Thy servant Jacob, after the wrestling of Penuel. So disarm them, for I do not know the length of Satan's chain in this case, and in this unbrotherly attack. But Thou canst shorten the chain as short as it may please Thee.

"Lord, I anticipate them in point of law. They think of casting Thine unworthy servant into the little courts here below; but I cast my cause into the High Court, in which Thou, gracious Jesus, art the High Chancellor. Receive Thou the cause of Thine unworthy servant and send him a writ, or a notice, immediately – sending into their conscience, and summoning them to consider what they are doing. Oh frighten them with a summons from Thy court until they come and bow in contrition at Thy feet; and take from their hands every revengeful weapon, and make them deliver up every gun of scandal, and every sword of bitter words, and every spear of slanderous expressions, and surrender them all at Thy cross.

"Forgive them all their faults, and clothe them with white robes, and give them oil for their heads, and the organ and harp of ten strings to sing, for the trampling of Satan under our feet by the God of peace."

Concerning this time he later wrote:

"I went up once and was about ten minutes in prayer; I felt some confidence that Jesus heard. I went up again with a tender heart; I could not refrain from weeping with the joy of hope that the Lord was drawing near to me.

After the seventh struggle I came down, fully believing that the Redeemer had taken my cause into His hands, and that He would arrange and manage for me. My countenance was cheerful as I came down the last time, like Naaman, having washed himself seven times in the Jordan; or Bunyan's pilgrim, having cast his burden at the foot of the cross into the grave of Jesus.

"I well remember the place – the little house adjoining the meeting house at Cildwrn, where I then resided – in which this struggle took place; I can call it Penuel. No weapon intended against me prospered, and I had peace at once to my mind and in my (temporal) condition. I have frequently prayed for those who would injure me that they might be blessed, even as I have been blessed."

Mercifully the threat was never executed, and he heard no more of the matter. How easy it is to begin to wonder *why* Christmas Evans should have had all this worry but he himself knew: "I know not what would have become of me had it not been for these furnaces in which I have been tried and in which the spirit of prayer has been excited and exercised in me."

He had now laboured so long and with so much blessing in Anglesey (apart from those called by grace under his preaching, twenty-eight men had begun themselves to preach) that it might have been thought that he would finish his days there. But clouds of trouble were now thickening round him. Severe eye trouble threatened completely to blind him, and for a period of nine months he was unable to preach, most of the time being spent in hospital at Aberystwyth. The churches, established under his ministry, to whom he was a father, grew restive and self-willed, resenting his guidance and refusing his advice. He had never enjoyed much of this world's goods or comforts, but he might have expected that his last days would be spent peacefully and joyfully among the churches for whom he had done so much. But it was not to be so.

MENAI STRAIT

Yet, though brought so low, he did not sink. He had never built his hopes on either the faithfulness of men or the spirituality of the churches. His hopes had a surer foundation, even Christ Himself. Also he had never been permitted to be carried away by the tremendous popularity he enjoyed; he was kept beneath the sacred influence of the truth he believed and preached. He had never sought popularity; rather that the truth might be blessed to those to whom he preached. So the Lord lifted him above grief, and disappointment, and unfriendliness, and the dictatorship and impertinence of deacons and church members.

Nevertheless, magnifying his office as a servant of the Most High God, he felt he could not yield to the spirit of turbulence and faction; and so at last he was compelled and constrained to leave. Thus this faithful ministry was removed from Anglesey and Anglesey soon (yet too late) regretted the removal.

"Everything," he wrote, "now conspired to induce my departure from the island: the unyielding spirit of those who had oppressed and traduced me; and my own state of mind fully believing that there was yet more work for me to do in the harvest of the Son of Man; my earnest prayers for divine guidance during one whole year, and the vision of my head at night in my bed – all worked together towards this result."

William Morgan, who had recently settled as the pastor at Holyhead, wrote:

> "It was an affecting sight to see the aged man, who had laboured so long and with such happy effects, leaving the sphere of his exertions under these circumstances; having laboured so much to pay for their meeting houses, having performed so many journeys to South Wales for their benefit, having served them so diligently in the island, and passed through so many dangers. Now some of the people withheld their contributions to avenge themselves on their own father in the gospel; others, while professing to be friends, did little more; while he, like David, was obliged to leave his city, not knowing whether he should ever return to see the ark of God and His tabernacle in Anglesey again.
>
> "Whatever misunderstanding there was between Mr. Evans and some of his brethren, it is clear that his counsels ought to have been received with due acknowledgment of his age and experience, and that his reputation should have been energetically vindicated. I am of opinion, I am quite convinced, that more strenuous

exertions should have been made to defend his character, and to bear him in the arms of love through the archers, and not to have permitted him to fall in the street without an advocate."

So in the year 1826 Christmas Evans left his beloved Anglesey, "cast down, but not destroyed." What was it that bore up his wounded spirit? He himself tells us: "Nothing could preserve me in cheerfulness and confidence under these afflictions but the assurance of the faithfulness of Christ"; and again: "As soon as I went into the pulpit during this period I forgot my troubles and found my mountain strong. I was blessed with such heavenly unction, and I felt the truth like a hammer in power, and the doctrine distilling like the honeycomb and like unto the rarest wine."

His reasons for leaving Anglesey were especially that the churches over which he was "overseer" began to assert their independence, appoint their own ministers (even against Christmas Evans's advice), and generally to resent his control. He was even accused of doctrinal unsoundness, and happenings of over thirty years before (and they were untrue!) were raised against him. We can understand the venerable minister being bitterly grieved and hurt. But infallibility belongs only to God; and it would seem clear that Christmas Evans – godly man, great man – was not always at his best in dealing with people and in organising, sometimes touchy or tactless. Also the system of church order he sought to perpetuate was a strange one: believing the churches were feeble, he would not agree to complete independency, but insisted on having a measure of control – a situation which could not continue for ever among Baptist churches. Even the best would not tolerate a Particular Baptist "pope."

CHAPTER 15

Caerphilly:
Abundant Blessing

"As Jacob left father and mother with staff only, so did I leave the church for which I had prayed and laboured for nearly forty years with none of this world's goods but the horse which I rode and a little money in my pocket, which I could scarcely call my own." So wrote Christmas Evans of his departure from Anglesey. We view him with sorrow – one of the most popular preachers that ever stood in a pulpit, now in the sixtieth year of his age, bereaved of his beloved wife, in shattered health and sorrow of spirit, wondering what direction to take.

He speaks in one of his sermons of days of loneliness and darkness:

"When I am weak, and distressed, and alone, and none to receive my tale of sorrow, none to express a word of fellow-feeling or of care for me, in the living oracles of the gospel I see divine wisdom and lovingkindness looking at me tenderly, compassionately, through the openings of my prison, and I feel that He who dresses the lily of the field, and numbers the sparrows, is near me, numbering the hairs of my head, listening to my cries, in all the treasures of His grace and power. He is the same gracious Redeemer and Preserver to every one that believes in His name."

Caerphilly (today mainly known for its cheese) was now to be the scene of his labours. It was a poor little village, lying in a mountain valley, when Christmas Evans went there. Yet it has its claim to fame. Caerphilly castle, now ruined, was once the largest in Britain next to Windsor. Here King Edward II retreated. From here he escaped in the disguise of a peasant, hiring himself as a farm labourer. Here at a later period Owain Glyndwr lived. For many years it was owned by the Spencer family, who plundered the local inhabitants, so that it became a symbol of gloom and horror – having an awful tower for prisoners, its walls of wonderful thickness.

How came it that Christmas Evans went to Caerphilly? It is said that, praying for an opening in providence, he was visited by a minister who said, "If you are definitely leaving Anglesey, I know of a place for you."

"What place is it?"

"Caerphilly."

"Caerphilly, Caerphilly; write at once and tell them I'll come to Caerphilly."

He had about two hundred miles to travel from Anglesey – a long, solitary journey. Yet he wrote:

"On my way from Llangefni to Brynsiencyn, I felt such tenderness of heart, and that Christ's presence was so near me, that as the coldness of my nature dissolved, I could not refrain from breaking out in supplications and tears. The wrestling lasted for some hours. I had strength given me to entrust myself and my ministry to Jesus Christ with a confidence that raised me above all my troubles."

It is almost impossible to realise the interest and excitement caused by his arrival. Until he actually arrived, there were some who believed he never could leave his beloved Anglesey. It is said that all kinds of people caught up the report.

"Christmas Evans is come!"

"Are you sure of it?"

"Yes, quite sure of it; he preached at Caerphilly last Sunday."

Taking up his abode in the chapel house, cared for by a housekeeper who knew nothing about his mode of life, he was not really happy. South Wales seemed so different to him from North Wales. His friends suggested that he should seek to be guided to another wife. It was even suggested that a person of wealth would be suitable. After a little reflection the reply was: "I tell you, it is my firm opinion that I am never to have any property in the soil of this world until I have a grave."

In the end the name of Mary Evans, the faithful housekeeper for himself and his late wife in Anglesey, was mentioned. This seemed to touch a cord. She was sent for (a faithful friend travelling with two saddled horses, and bringing her back with joy) and soon became his wife, taking excellent care of him till his dying day. The marriage took place at Eglwysilian church, in the same parish where George Whitefield had been married.

Christmas Evans himself gives a few interesting details of his personal life at this time:

"My health is good, although I have broken one of my legs, which is painless and is mending well. Every month I preach in the following houses in the neighbourhood: Mr. Llewellyn, Bedwas; Mr. Jenkins, Rhydri, a rich man converted from drink since I came here, and a constant listener but not yet a member – but he has asked for a monthly preaching service in his home. I preach in another house near Taff's Well and in the chapel there every Thursday. One great advantage of this house preaching is that I do not go out to the cold air in perspiration, a great comfort to an old man.

"Mr. Jones of Pontypridd has given me sufficient hay to feed my pony for this year of scarcity. It is likely that the little one will become a thousand and the weak a strong race.

"I have no desire to return to Anglesey. Mrs. Evans has renewed her youth and is full of her first love – she sings as in the days of old. She talks of spiritual things all day long and never tires."

His salary was now £40 a year (77p a week), and his house free from rent or rates. It was under the same roof as the chapel. In addition there was a small field in which to keep his pony.

His ministry at Caerphilly was abundantly blessed. There was such an unction upon his ministry and the sanctifying effect of the deep sorrows through which he had passed was clearly witnessed. He wrote:

"The Spirit descended upon the church at Caerphilly, and we united to seek in the name of Christ an outpouring of divine influence."

He was still a dreamer, and at the start of his Caerphilly pastorate he had had a striking dream. He found himself in a chapel like Caerphilly, and hanging from the roof were many harps in green coverings, whilst in the background the devil was anxiously watching them, as if trembling for his own kingdom. The dreamer said, "I'll reach down those heavenly harps," and doing so cried out, "Bless the Lord for He has visited us according to His promises and our prayers and expectations." In two years, such was God's blessing resting on the Word, that some hundred and forty members were added by baptism to the church. This, he believed, was the interpretation and fulfilling of the vision of the harps.

Caerphilly became as "a city set on a hill." Every Sabbath multitudes might be seen wending their way to chapel across the hills from every side, and it has been said that those who knew Christmas Evans stated that his preaching at this period surpassed anything that had been heard before. His preaching was the topic of conversation in hundreds of homes each Sabbath evening. Neighbours would hear from those who had been to Caerphilly what wonderful truths had been spoken. So there was a witness, both in the district, and through much of Glamorgan and Monmouth. It would appear that many young people especially were influenced by the power of the truth, leaving the haunts of pleasure which had been their delight.

Two young men who were abundantly blessed at this time under Christmas Evans's preaching, Caleb Edmunds and Morgan Evans, seemed destined to great usefulness in the church of God – but one died just after commencing his first pastorate and the other without having even commenced a pastoral charge.

There were also older people, some of whom had been drunkards, and the publicans complained that their trade had decreased considerably since Christmas Evans came into the district.

CAERPHILLY CASTLE

It was at this time that a dying minister, J. P. Davies of Tredegar, had to spend a few months under medical care at Caerphilly. He passed much time with Christmas Evans and was delighted with his company and astonished by the fulness and blessedness of his ministry Sabbath by Sabbath, this being a real comfort during his last days.

In after years the inhabitants of the district used to reckon things that happened by Christmas Evans's sermons. "It must have happened then because that was the time when Christmas Evans preached 'The Wedding Ring' sermon."

But besides his reputation as a great preacher, Christmas Evans had also gained the reputation of being an eminently godly man. Two well-known stories that are told of him are typical of the godliness of his character.

93

On one occasion he employed a man to sell his old horse for him at a horse fair. After a time Christmas Evans called to see what was happening, and found that the bargain was almost completed.

"Is this your horse, Mr. Evans?" said the purchaser.

"Certainly it is," he replied.

"What is his age, sir?"

"Twenty-three years."

"But this man tells me he is only fifteen!"

"He is certainly twenty-three, for he has been with me these twenty years, and he was three years old when I bought him."

"Is he safe-footed?"

"No, he is far from that. Indeed, that is why I want to part with him – and he has never been put into harness either since I bought him."

The dealer in vain tried to stop him, whispering that he would never be able to sell the horse. But in this he was mistaken for the buyer, intrigued by Christmas Evans's integrity, paid a very handsome price. And, somehow, the whole story got round Wales.

The other story is of a minister who treated Christmas Evans most unkindly. Soon afterwards this minister was charged with a crime and taken to court. On the day of the trial Christmas Evans went aside in secret and pleaded with God that his old foe might be upheld, and his name cleared. With what delight did he hear the news that he had been acquitted. He was with a company of ministers at the time, but, with tears in his eyes, he immediately fell on his knees, exclaiming, "Thanks be unto Thee, O Lord Jesus, for delivering one of Thy servants from the mouth of the lions."

CHAPTER 16

Cardiff:

Change and Decay

It may seem strange (and yet really is not so) that after leaving Anglesey Christmas Evans never remained in any place long: Caerphilly, 1826–1828; Cardiff, 1828–1832; Caernarfon, 1832–1838. His life in Anglesey, together with the unusualness of both his gifts and character, had not really prepared him for more restricted labour. He was called to preach in different conditions at a time in his life when he was least suited to change. Hence a new home and pastorate seemed surrounded with unusual difficulties and the brief stays which made up the remainder of his life were only what could have been expected. Moreover, he tended to look on his removal both to Caerphilly and to Cardiff in the light of a preaching mission.

Yet it would seem his popularity was maintained. A chapel service, where he had been announced some weeks before, has been graphically described:

"With the full dawn there is set in motion an untiring crowd, many of whom follow the preacher the whole of the day. Wherever he goes, thither the multitude follows from village to village, leaving the other chapels to bear unmistakeable evidence that something unusual is going on elsewhere. But in the evening something greater still is expected: the chapel will be larger; there will be no other services in the neighbourhood; and the crisis of the excitement is sure to come on. So in they troop from all points of the compass towards the central place, small groups of people heralding the way full two hours before the time; for nothing is more certain than that, come what may, there will not even be standing room for the crowds that will assemble.

"In half-an-hour more the roads look picturesque and lively with all sorts of people, some on foot, others on horseback, all wending their way towards the chapel; and while so doing, communicating their wonder at what they had already heard, and their still growing expectations. By five o'clock, an hour before the time, the place is crowded with people, who wait patiently, still with restless expectation, for the advent of the preacher. Still the numbers swell, and no one word, as generally used, will describe the scene before us. Every effort is made to pack the people as closely as possible, which can be better done perhaps as there are no pews in the way. The process of wedging is accomplished to a perfection known only to a Welsh congregation. The seats are all densely occupied, but there is room for a standing row in front of each, and for another standing array on the seats already seemingly filled, and the spectacle presented is that of a triple row, accommodated under the pressure of ingenious necessity within the space usually assigned to one. But what does it signify, if they can only hear? The place becomes intensely hot; the windows are all thrown open; some of them bodily removed; still the people press forward for admission, and occupy aisles, stairs and entrance, leaving out of doors an eager, inadmissible multitude."

Concerning leaving Caerphilly he wrote:

"I never spent a short time more comfortably, as the ark of God had appeared there, and (referring to his dream) the harmony of some hundred and forty harps had been heard among us. I would gladly have spent my days there, but was not permitted to do so on account of some things respecting which I was not to blame. I still love many of the brethren and sisters there and wish them prosperity, and desire that neither their faults nor my own may appear against us in the day of judgment; but that we may be graciously brought to confess our sins upon the earth, where the fountain of forgiveness has been opened."

The point was that the Caerphilly deacons and church members were used to controlling things themselves – a situation Christmas Evans could not for a moment brook. There seems to have been a reluctance to give him the scriptural authority of a pastor.

CARDIFF CASTLE

In deliberating his move, when travelling over the Caerphilly mountains from Tongwynlais, a spirit of prayer descended on him. He says:

> "I wept for hours, supplicating Jesus Christ . . . While on the mountains I had a deep sense of nearness to Christ; I felt as if He were close by me."

At this time he entered into one of those solemn covenants (which he later wrote out when at Cardiff). Amongst other things these were his desires:

> "1. Grant me the favour of being led according to Thy will, by the intimations of Thy providence and Thy word, and my own personal desires as inclined by Thy Spirit; for the sake of Thine infinitely precious blood. Amen. – C.E.

> "4. Suffer me not to be trampled under the foot of pride by members or deacons, for the sake of Thy goodness, O Lord. Amen. – C.E. (pathetic, in a special way!)

> "5. Vouchsafe unto me the inestimable favour of being in Thine hand the means of reclaiming sinners to Thyself, and of edifying Thy people wherever Thou mayest send me; for Thy name's sake. Amen. – C.E.

> "9. Cherish Thou me beneath the shadow of Thy sympathy, which can 'be touched with a feeling of our infirmity,' and Thy boundless power 'to succour them that are tempted.' Amen. – C.E.

> "10. Accept of my million thanksgivings that Thou hast not hitherto cast me away as a darkened star, or 'like a vessel wherein is no pleasure,' and suffer me not to outlive my usefulness. Amen. – C.E. Thanks be unto Thee, that Thou hast 'not given me as a prey to the teeth of the enemy.'"

Coming to Cardiff he said he felt "like a merchant

who, having insured his vessel, has nothing to lose; for I had committed myself to Jesus, the Mediator of the new testament, for time and eternity."

But there were great difficulties at Cardiff. The previous pastor had, by immoral behaviour, disgraced both himself and the church yet, strangely, he remained in the town and still attended the chapel. Christmas Evans, blessed with discernment, soon came to the conclusion that he was a man destitute of grace, and could see no sign of repentance. Some considered him very harsh; but, in the fear of God, he stood firm, and the following years solemnly proved he was not deceived.

Whilst at Cardiff, having more time on his hands, he began to prepare a volume of his sermons for the press even though his eye was very weak, and prayed concerning them:

"The sermons I am preparing for the press, let them be to Thy praise, and not mine. To Thee I dedicate them. If there be anything in them to Thy glory, and of service to Thy kingdom, do Thou take charge of it, and make it known unto men; otherwise let it perish like a drop of a bucket in the scorching heat of Africa.

"O grant that a drop of that water, which Thou alone canst give, and which springs up to eternal life, may run through all my sermons."

Again he prayed,

"And I now come unto Thee, O Lord, to have Thy counsel whether or not to proceed with the work. Is it a part of my duty, or is it a foolish, useless notion of my own? I implore, for Thy name's sake, Thy gracious guidance. With my failing eyesight, let me not perplex myself with a work which Thou wilt not bless, and which will be buried in oblivion. If Thou wilt not open a door for me (for Thou hast the keys of the house of David) in Thy providence, that I may obtain names to enable me to bring the work through the press without the risk of debt and disgrace, if Thou, the Great Shepherd of the sheep, wilt not enable me to hold forth the true gospel, not only without error, but also with the savour and unction of the works of Bunyan and the hymns of Williams (which Thou art likely to bless as long as Thou hast a church in Wales), if they will not be to Thy glory in the building up of Thy people and the conversion of sinners, do Thou incline me to lay the work aside. If Thou wilt take it under Thy direction and care, strengthen me to carry out the design. Thou knowest, O Lord, that I feel my insignificance for the task, and my utter unworthiness even to ask such a favour of Thee, but I cannot refrain from placing these petitions before Thee; therefore, for the sake of Thine infinite merits, according to Thy word unto Thy people, grant me my request. Amen."

A number of hymns he wrote were also published at this time, hymns of profound depth which touch the foundations of vital godliness.

More and more now he withdrew himself in communion with his God; almost whole days and portions of his nights he spent in prayer. Removed from his old associations and feeling many infirmities of old age growing on him, he increasingly felt the value of the secret place. Yet during the less than four years he spent at Cardiff about eighty members were added to the church.

Like George Whitefield Christmas Evans often preached a sermon several times. His sermon on 1 Timothy 3. 16 was one which he preached on more than one occasion: "Without controversy great is the mystery of godliness: God was manifest in the flesh, justified in the Spirit, seen of angels, preached unto the

Gentiles, believed on in the world, received up into glory." It was during his Cardiff pastorate that his biographer Rhys Stephen heard him preach it at Tredegar (about the year 1830) and says: "While I have the faintest trace of memory as to sermons I may have heard, this must always be prominent and distinct. In its oratorical excellence it stands alone, even among his great achievements."

Apart from the oratory some portions are particularly beautiful and sacred.

But there were still the difficulties, and sadly there were two or three wealthy men and women who were thorns in their minister's side. The churches in Anglesey had fought for democracy and others throughout Wales contended for the same – only to find it not true New Testament independency but, so often, a wealthy oligarchy stealing power for themselves. So his prayer at this time was: "I would hide beneath the shadow of Thy wings. Hide me in the secret place of Thy pavilion from the strife of tongues."

At an Association meeting in 1832 it was decided he should go to Caernarfon, though he had received several invitations. The cordial reception he received at the Association did much to revive him, and everything was done to comfort and honour him. Yet it was said that his preaching did not seem to have the same authority and power now, except on occasions.

Some of his Liverpool friends kindly presented the old man with the gift of a gig. (These friends included William Rushton, the author of *A Defence of Particular Redemption* – an answer to Andrew Fuller.) Henceforth he always travelled by gig – so returning to Cardiff, he preached his last sermon and with his old horse now harnessed to the new vehicle, he slowly travelled to Caernarfon for the evening of his life.

Looking back over an interesting and eventful life he gave a quaint but typical summary of it not long before leaving Cardiff:

"It appears to me only as yesterday when I first went into Anglesey, my wife with me, on a day of unusual frost and snow. 'I will remember thee from the land of Jordan, and of the Hermonites, from the hill Mizar.' I remember the battles which I fought there; the powder and the fiery bolts of prayers and sermons; the sword, the bow and the arrow, the shield and the buckler, on the fields of Brynsiencyn, Llangefni, etc.; the prisoners of war that were taken, and the arms and ammunition of the enemy that fell into the hands of the army of Emmanuel. I remember the march-tunes which we used to sing on our way to and from the field of battle. I cannot but remember, with mingled feelings, those eminent officers who led the unconquerable hosts of the Methodists of those days, in Anglesey and Carnarvonshire, not less men than the seraphic Robert Roberts, of Llanllyfni, Evan Richard, the sweet singer of Carnarvon, and the gifted John Jones, of Edeyrn; but they have all retired, and I am still on the field, having fought the battles of Copenhagen and Waterloo in Glamorganshire. The distant echoes of our march-tunes, in Llŷn and Anglesey, still sound in my ears, and I have a black book in which are graved the names of the betrayers with a 'pen of iron and lead'; and the names of those who turned not back in the day of battle are written in the book of 'the white stone and the new name' with the red ink that flows from the rock of Calvary.

"Since I resigned the command in Anglesey, I have been looking out for fields which most required an old field-marshal, who knows how, through God, to handle as of old the sword and the bow. I took some part in the wars at Caerphilly, and by the mighty arm of the God of

Jacob, some hundred and forty prisoners of war were led captive under the banner of Emmanuel, and they were enlisted in His army in the course of a two years' campaign, as vigorous as any I ever saw. After that, the old field-marshal went to Cardiff, where the army was in the greatest danger, its leader having been shot down by great Diabolus. The divine power, upon which the old field-marshal relies, took here again some scores of prisoners of war, and I trust they will be sustained in the new army to the end.

"My plan since leaving Anglesey, where I was for nearly forty years, is to go to those places where there is required an old reaper, an old mower, as well as an old warrior; and to go on cheerfully as long as the army and the sub-officers submit to the King's laws, and do not frown upon me and 'turn into their own ways' instead of listening to their superior who, like a shepherd, shows them the way, as Evangelist did to the pilgrim."

CHAPTER 17

Caernarfon: Last Days

Who can doubt that Christmas Evans welcomed the opportunity to return to the north? Caernarfon and Anglesey were almost one; he had but to cross the Menai Strait to be again in Anglesey, the scene of his many trials and deliverances, his spiritual conflicts and trials. And in reality he had been away only six years – though so much seemed to have happened in that time.

His return to his old neighbourhood created universal delight. (At this period a feature of Welsh religious life was the almost incredible affection shown to aged ministers.) The first Sabbath brought together a large multitude of people, many more than the chapel could hold. There was a congregation outside many times as large as the one inside so the new minister took his place at the window, whence he could address the vast audience. The great excitement continued, large congregations assembling on the Lord's day and in the week. In the town itself he was treated with the utmost respect, from both church and chapel.

But the circumstances themselves were very unfavourable – the church itself small; burdened by squabbles and disputes; and, of course, the usual debt.

The ancient city of Caernarfon was well suited to inspire the rich imagery of his sermons: the castle; the dangerous coast; the new Menai Bridge* eight miles away, completed by Telford only in 1826; the wild beauty of the scenery. Even the lighthouse off the coast he uses:

"I was once told by a man who kept a lighthouse between Anglesey and Ireland that on dark and tempestous nights multitudes of birds, having lost their way and seeking for shelter, flew wildly against it, and were found dead in the morning. So, many souls, who have not 'lodged in the branches of the great tree' before the night came, driven by the storm of death, strike against the great lighthouse of Sinai's law, seeking shelter, but in vain."

The horrors of shipwreck were sometimes dwelt on. It is said that on one occasion he described the scene so dramatically that his hearers almost fancied they were sinking into the deep – the helplessness of the foundering bark, the sinner; then the life-boat, the rescue, salvation in Christ.

After his settlement in Caernarfon he often preached at monthly meetings in the district and several times at the Associations, even in the south. He threw himself enthusiastically into the temperance movement, and found time to produce *Lectures on the Apocalypse.*

*Work started in 1819, and the suspension bridge was opened on January 30th, 1826, the first vehicle to cross being the London to Holyhead royal mail coach. It cost £120,000. (£25,000 was paid in compensation to the owner of the nearest ferry.)

At the end of his first year in Caernarfon he wrote:

"I have much cause to thank God for His grace to me in this place. Many things are better than they were twelve months ago. All was then a desolate wilderness – yea, the dwelling place of dragons;"

but he continued:

"Oh, it is most difficult to raise again a fallen cause! for Satan has a double advantage in this town – gathering disgrace from the immorality of professors, and thence manufacturing continuous objections to the discredit of religion."

CAERNARFON CASTLE

His last years were happy ones. He now revisited his former scenes of labour. Soon after his return to the north, an Association meeting was held at Llangefni in a field close to Cildwrn cottage itself. Once more he stood upon the sacred spot. The whole neighbourhood turned out to see the old patriarch again. And the preacher was just the same, or even richer, mellowed with age. It was the old Christmas Evans. Old memories were revived; old wounds healed; and the old love to their old pastor and father in Christ was rekindled. Aged men and women recalled the time when he first came to the island and that wonderful period of change that had taken place.

He preached at ten o'clock in the morning; and as groups of people made their way from every part of the island, the past was revived as the texts and sermons of past days were remembered, and the wonders of God's free grace.

When he stood up to preach there was quite a commotion. After a verse had been sung he announced his text: "And so will I go in unto the King, which is not according to the law; and if I perish, I perish." His introduction was brief and his emotions restrained as he opened up the text. He began:

> "I am happy and thankful that I am once again privileged to visit the country of my prayers. It is the same treasure chest I have as of old, and the same treasure as contents ('the Lamb slain')."

Then there was a display of eloquence worthy of his best days. When, towards the close, he referred to his own past in Anglesey, to well-known preachers who had entered into rest, and to the probability that they should see his face no more, the tears flowed freely. This was almost certainly the occasion when one who wept profusely was the renowned John Elias, who sat three yards away from the platform.

It was at this time, when musing on the past, that he

was brought to admire the faithfulness of his God to him through a long life:

> "I have been thinking of the great goodness of the Lord unto me throughout my unworthy ministry; and now, in my old age, I see the work prospering wonderfully in my hand, so that there is reason to think that I am, in some degree, a blessing to the church when I might have been a burden to it, or rather a curse, by which one might have been induced to wish me laid in the earth that I might no longer prevent the progress of the work. Thanks be to God that it is not so! Though I deserve no better, yet I am in the land of mercy. This is unto me according to the manner of God unto His people. My path in the valley, the dangers, and the precipices of destruction upon which I have stood, rush into my thoughts, and also the sinking of many in death, and the downfall of others by immorality and their burial in Kibroth-Hattaavah, the graves of inordinate desire, together with the withering, the feebleness and the unfruitfulness of some through the influence of a secret departure from God, and of walking in the hidden paths that lead to apostasy."

But it was hard work at Caernarfon, what with the debt and the poverty of the people. £800 was the debt when Christmas Evans arrived in Caernarfon and though half had now been raised, the remainder still hung about their necks like a millstone, and the time had come when the whole remaining sum needed to be paid.

So the burden once more fell upon the preacher. Was it possible that, at his advanced age, he could still venture on a begging tour? There seemed no other way. Go he must. So it must be that the closing scene shall be in harmony with the journeys of days long past.

CHAPTER 18

"Drive On!"

We come to Christmas Evans's last preaching tour – yet once again to raise money for a needy chapel. There was still a debt of £400 on his own chapel in Caernarfon, and the people were poor. So once again the old man started forth on a tour of the south in an attempt to raise the sum. It was in April 1838 that he set off, along with his wife and a young preacher named John Hughes.

Before he commenced he sent a touching circular letter to God's people in the south of Wales. In it he said:

> "The term of the lease of life has expired in my case, even threescore and ten years, and I am very much afflicted. I am purposed to sacrifice myself to this object, though I am afraid I shall die on the journey . . . O brethren, pray with me for protection on the journey – for strength and health *this once* on occasion of my bidding farewell to you all! Pray for the light of the Lord's countenance upon me

in preaching; pray for His own glory, and that His key may open the hearts of the people to contribute towards His cause. O help us, brethren! . . . This is my last sacrifice for the Redeemer's cause."

And it did prove to be his last journey; he did die without returning home.

But what an itinerary was planned! A task enough for the strongest man in the prime of life:

"May 1838: Tuesday 1st, Dolgellau; Wednesday 2nd, Dolgellau; Thursday 3rd, Machynlleth; Friday 4th, Talywern; Sunday 6th, Trefnewydd; Tuesday 8th, Caersws; Wednesday 9th, Llanidloes; Thursday 10th, Capel Newydd; Sunday 13th, Nantgwyn 10 a.m., Dolau 6 p.m.; Tuesday 15th, Pontnewydd; Wednesday 16th, Llanfair; Thursday 17th, Brecon; Sunday 20th, Maesyberllan 10 a.m., Brecon 6 p.m.; Monday 21st, Llangynidr; Tuesday 22nd, John Edwards's Chapel; Wednesday 23rd, Nantyglo; Thursday 24th, Horeb, Blaenavon; Friday 25th, Ebenezer, Blaenavon; Sunday 27th, Llanwenarth 10 a.m., Llanelli 6 p.m.; Monday 28th, Pontypool; Tuesday 29th, Trosnant; Wednesday 30th, Abersychan; Thursday 31st, Pontrhydyrun.

"June: Friday 1st, Gwaith Newydd; Sunday 3rd, Newport; Tuesday 5th, Beulah; Wednesday 6th, Argoed; Thursday 7th, Penycae; Friday 8th, Tredegar; Sunday 10th, Sirhowy 10 a.m., Tredegar 6 p.m.; Monday 11th, Rhymney; Tuesday 12th, Dowlais; Wednesday 13th, Seion, Merthyr; Thursday 14th, Ebenezer, Merthyr; Friday 15th, Hirwaun; Sunday 17th, Seion, Merthyr 10 a.m., Ebenezer, Merthyr 6 p.m.; Monday 18th, Aberdare; Tuesday 19th, Pontypridd; Wednesday 20th, Hengoed; Thursday

21st, Caerphilly; Friday 22nd, Y Groeswen; Sunday 24th, Caerphilly; Monday 25th, Ffwrwm Eistedd; Tuesday 26th, Risca; Wednesday 27th, Castleton; Thursday 28th, Caerleon; Friday 29th, Bethel.

"July: Sunday 1st, Basaleg 10 a.m., Castleton 6 p.m.; Monday 2nd, Llaneurwg; Tuesday 3rd, Cardiff; Wednesday 4th, Whitchurch; Sunday 8th, Cardiff; Monday 9th, Pontfaen; Tuesday 10th, Bridgend; Wednesday 11th, Aberavon; Thursday 12th, Neath; Friday 13th, Swansea; Sunday 15th, Swansea."

As he passed along he was received with great joy; perhaps he was never so well loved as now. Wherever he preached, the place was thronged at an early hour and multitudes remained outside, unable to gain admittance. The money began to flow in.

He reached Monmouthshire, where he preached a remarkable sermon before the county Association on the text: "By grace are ye saved." But the effort was too much for him, and he was laid up for a week. Loving friends did all they could to make him happy and comfortable. During this time he was very bright in spirits, and loved to speak of the gospel, especially concerning the safety of every believer:

> "'This is the gospel,' he said. 'He that believeth shall be saved.' Now, in order to the truth of this declaration, every believer must be saved. If in the last day the great enemy find one single soul not saved who ever believed the gospel, he would take that soul up, present that soul to the Judge and to the immense assembly, and say, 'The gospel is not true.' He would take that lost believer through all the regions of pandemonium, and exhibit him in triumph to the devils and the damned. No, *never! never! never!*"

Leaving Tredegar, somewhat recovered, at the end

of the week, he went on his way preaching at Caerphilly, Cardiff, Cowbridge, Bridgend and Neath, reaching Swansea on the Saturday, July 14th. The next day he preached twice ("like a seraph," one of his hearers said), in the morning on the prodigal son, and in the evening: "I am not ashamed of the gospel of Christ." He was the guest of a blind preacher, Daniel Davies.

On the Monday evening he preached (in English) on the text: "Beginning at Jerusalem." He was very feeble and was never his happiest when preaching in English. On this occasion he seemed particularly tried. Yet there was much beauty in his discourse:

> "Beginning at Jerusalem! Why at Jerusalem? The apostles were to begin there because its inhabitants had been witness to the life and death of Christ; there He had preached, wrought miracles, been crucified, and rose again. Here, on the very spot of His deepest degradation, He was also to be exalted. He had been crucified as a malefactor, He was now to be elevated in the same place as a King. Here were accorded to Him the first-fruits of His resurrection."

This was the strain of his sermon:

> "'At Jerusalem, Lord?' 'Yes.' 'Why, Lord, these are the men who crucified Thee; we are not to preach it to *them*?' 'Yes, preach it to all' . . . 'Suppose we meet the very man that nailed Thy hands and feet to the cross, the very man that pierced Thy side, that spat in Thy face?' 'Preach the gospel to them all: tell them all that I am the Saviour; I am the same Lord over all, and rich unto all that call upon Me.'"

As he came down the pulpit steps, he could be heard murmuring, "This is my last sermon!" And so it was.

During the night he was taken very ill. The next day he was worse, and the day following worse still. A doctor had to be called. Yet on the Thursday he was able to get up, and even had a walk in the garden. That night he was worse again.

On the Friday morning he said to those around his bed: "I am leaving you. I have laboured in the sanctuary fifty-three years, and this is my comfort, that I have never laboured without blood in the basin" (this being, of course, a beautiful reference to the Passover, Exodus chapter 12, especially verse 22). The great theme of his preaching was his hope in death – to find shelter beneath the precious blood of Christ.

He continued:

"Preach Christ to the people, brethren."

Then, his dying testimony:

"Look at me. In myself I am nothing but ruin, but in Christ I am heaven and salvation."

He repeated a verse from a favourite Welsh hymn:

> "Dyma'r wisg ddisglaerwen eleu,
>   Guddia'm noethni hyd y llawr;
> Fel nad ofnwyf byth ymddangos
>   Mwy o flaen dy orsedd fawr;"

which, roughly translated, reads:

> "This the robe so bright and glorious,
>   O'er my naked spirit thrown;
> So that I no longer tremble
>   To appear before Thy throne."

So he died as he had lived, trusting in the righteousness of Christ.

Then, as if done with earth, he waved his hand, and exclaimed, "GOODBYE! DRIVE ON!" Was he again, in his thoughts, travelling alone with his faithful pony

"DRIVE ON!"

over the lonely mountains? Was it another instance of the labour of life being uppermost in the moment of death?

"Goodbye! Drive on!" But now it is another journey – from earth to heaven. He turned over and seemed to sleep, but it was a sleep from which he never awoke on earth. It was July 19th, 1838, in the seventy-third year of his life, and the fifty-fourth of his ministry.

There was sorrow throughout Wales, especially in his beloved Anglesey. And it is said there never was such a funeral in Swansea, crowds of mourners weeping their way to the grave, following one who to them had been a father. "There is a prince and a great man fallen in Israel."

Death did not take him by surprise. He was ready. At times he had gloomy thoughts but the Lord showed

him the remedy – nothing in self, all in Christ.
This was his testimony:

> "When I yield to pensive reflections under a sense of sin,
> and when I see the tops of dark mountains of disease and
> tremble at the terrors of the grave, I see in the Bible
> infinite goodness, fairer than the Shekinah of old, looking
> at me out of eternity. It is like the smile of the eternal
> King from His throne of mercy. Divine love, the merits of
> Christ, the riches of grace, they are all here, and they
> assure me, and I listen to the still small voice that follows
> in this train until I feel myself lifted up out of the cave of
> despair by the dark mountain, and I stand on my feet."

Epilogue

In the first half of the last century a most interesting picture was published. It consisted of the portraits of the heads of seventy-five men: all ministers, all Baptists, all famous. One can imagine this picture, bearing the title "Baptist Messenger Memorial Portraits" hanging on the walls of Victorian homes and being gazed at with admiration. (This old picture has recently been reproduced in *The Sword and Trowel.*)

There they are: from Kiffin, Knollys, Keach and Bunyan onwards; the Stennetts; Dr. Gill (in the most honoured position in the centre); then Swain, Medley, Abraham Booth, Carey, Ryland; right down to William Gadsby. And conspicuous among them is Christmas Evans, squeezed in between two doctors of divinity.

We take it the picture is meant to contain the best-known and most-honoured ministers down to the time of its being issued. And "the one-eyed preacher of Wales" rightly deserves a place. Some, no doubt, had

116

more intellectual gifts and more ability as a writer; but surely none was more dearly loved and none more willing to sacrifice and be abased that Christ might be exalted.

David Rhys Stephen, his biographer, who preached at his funeral, said of him:

> "He had a heart swelling with love to God and man. Before the Highest he was ever prostrate, ever devout. He was a man that feared the Lord God of heaven and earth. He walked before Him with great humility all the day long. He had a deep and abiding sense of the awful character of our relation to God and eternity; and toward that God, and in reference to that eternity, he ever deported himself with reverence and fear. This gave a profoundness to his whole bearing as a preacher of the Word which was most exemplary and most impressive. His love to his fellow-men was manifested in the devotion of his long life to the service of his country, and to the edification of the church of God in it."

Concerning greatness as a preacher it is hard to fix a measure; but if the measure is sound doctrine, oratorical gifts, crowds who hear, and blessing that attends, then Christmas Evans was certainly not least among his brethren.

For many years he has largely been forgotten or, if known, remembered just for his quaintness – but he was both a very gracious and even great man. His own estimation, of course, was far different: like Paul, "Less than the least."

There are, of course, many lessons we can learn from his life:

1. The preaching that God has always blessed is the gospel that Christmas Evans preached, the "old-fashioned theology" of sin and salvation: "I determined

not to know any thing among you, save Jesus Christ and Him crucified."

2. God Himself sovereignly raises up men, equips them and uses them. They are all different and must not be imitated, especially in their peculiarities. Much harm was done by men trying to ape Christmas Evans.

3. The best of men are only men at best; no man is perfect.

4. What a wonderful example Christmas Evans has left us of humility and self-denial – no sacrifice too great for his beloved Lord and Master!

5. Only the same divine power that attended Christmas Evans's preaching can bring revival today. There is no substitute.

* * *

"Behold Lazarus lying in the cave, locked in the sleep of death. Now how shall he be raised? How shall he be brought back to life? Who will roll away for us the stone from the sepulchre? First came one who went down into the cold cave with blankets and salt to rub with the fomentations of duty, to appeal to the will, to say to the sleeping man that he *could* if he *would*. Chafing and rubbing the cold and inert limbs, he thinks to call back the vital warmth; and then retiring, and standing some distance apart, he says to the other spectators, 'Do you not see him stir? Are there no signs of life? Is he not moving?' No, he lies very still, there is no motion. How could it be otherwise? How could a sense of moral duty be felt by the man there? – *for the man was dead.*

"The first man gave up in despair. He had failed. Then came the second as cocksure as the first. 'I thought you would never do it,' he said with sarcasm. 'But if you look at me and watch carefully, you will see a thing or two. You have not learned the way yet. Your treatment was far too gentle.' And he went down into the cave with a scourge. With boastfulness he said, 'The man only wants severe treatment to be brought back to life. I will certainly make him feel.' And he laid on in quick succession the fervid blows, the sharp threatenings of law and judgment, and future danger and doom; and then he retired to some distance. 'Is he not waking?' he said. 'Do you not see the corpse stir?' No! A corpse he was before the man began to lay on his lashes, and a corpse he continued still – *for the man was dead.*

"'Ah,' said a third person as he advanced with head in air, 'I have wonderful power. You, with your rubbing and smiting, what can you do? You have nothing. I have two things, two vital things.' He advanced and fixed an electric battery, and arranged it so that it touched the dead man, and then from a flute which he held, he drew forth such sweet sounds that they charmed the ears which were listening; and whether it was the battery or whether it was the music, so it was that effect seemed to be produced. 'Behold,' said he, 'what the refinements of education and cultivation will do!' And, indeed, so it was, for the hair of the dead man seemed to rise, and his eyeballs seemed to start and dilate; and see! He rises, starts up, and takes a stride down the cave. Ah, but it is all over; it was nothing but the electricity in the battery; and he sank back again flat on the floor of the cave – *for the man was dead.*

"And then, when all were filled with despair, there came One, and stood by the entrance of the cave; but He was the Lord and Giver of life, and standing there, He said, 'Come from the four winds, O breath, and breathe upon this slain one, that he may live. Christ hath given thee life. Awake thou that sleepest!' And the man arose; he shook off his grave-clothes; what he needed had come to him now – *life!*

"*Life is the only cure for death.* Not the prescriptions of duty! Not the threats of punishment and damnation! Not the arts and the refinements of education! *But new, spiritual, divine life.*"

PRINTED BY ELPHICK COLOUR PRINT, BEDFORD, ENGLAND